MEDICAL
APOLOGETICS

THE UNIVERSE DIAGNOSED

KRIS F. FRENCH, MD

WESTBOW
PRESS®
A DIVISION OF THOMAS NELSON
& ZONDERVAN

WestBow Press books may be ordered through booksellers or by contacting:

WestBow Press
A Division of Thomas Nelson & Zondervan
1663 Liberty Drive
Bloomington, IN 47403
www.westbowpress.com
1 (866) 928-1240

ISBN: 978-1-5127-7882-3 (sc)
ISBN: 978-1-5127-7883-0 (hc)
ISBN: 978-1-5127-7881-6 (e)

Library of Congress Control Number: 2017903979

Print information available on the last page.

WestBow Press rev. date: 04/27/2017

DEDICATION

This book is dedicated to the Great Physician, the Creator who diagnoses, restores, and heals. The Creator who has disclosed Himself to us and blessed us with His son and creation so that we may glorify Him. He has blessed me with my family including my wife, Lindsey, and my three wonderful children, Klaire, James, and Frank.

CONTENTS

FORWARD

There are at least three reasons why I believe you should read this book. First, if you are not a scientist or a doctor you probably feel like me, intimidated and sometimes confused when it comes to understanding how science and the pursuit of God intersect. Dr. French does a fantastic job of using his medical expertise to help us understand that God and science are not in opposition to each other. Secondly, this book will expand your thinking and personal contemplations regarding who God is. While reading the book, there were multiple times where I was compelled to pause due to being filled with a sense of awe and wonder regarding the magnificence of the Creator and His creation. This book was good for my soul! Lastly, read this book because of the character and integrity of the author. For years, I have known Dr. French and have been deeply impressed at the way he lives out his beliefs and integrates his spirituality and his practice of medicine. This is the type of man I want to learn from. If you are like me, you often feel a bit under-qualified in the area of science and medicine. This sense of intimidation can make us feel as if there is a vast chasm between our contemplations about God and the scientific world. Because of this, our tendency is to separate the world of science and theology. Dr. French does a marvelous job bringing the two together in an integrated and comprehensible fashion. This book affirms the idea that Christianity is indeed a reasonable faith and excites me to learn more regarding how neurology and theology both inspire a sense of awe regarding the nature of the Creator. Dr. French applies his specific neurological training to the question of God. Using the accepted medical approach of observation, interpretation of data and diagnosis, he helps his readers to broaden their perspectives regarding the reality of God's existence.

As I read this book, I found myself filled with a sense of awe regarding the vastness and beauty of the Creator. Dr. French gives me confidence to think critically and to worship passionately.

- Nate Poetzl, Lead Pastor of Faith Chapel, Billings, Montana

INTRODUCTION

When I observe Your heavens, the work of Your fingers, the moon and the stars, which You set in place, what is man that You remember him, the son of man that You look after him?

—Psalm 8:3–4

The Bible teaches that human beings are valued among all God's creation. Humans have conscience and dignity. No matter what naturalists say about human beings being just another animal that can be self-aware due to evolution, we are not satisfied with that answer. Human beings are not just another part of nature; they have been called to steward it. There is something more than just this place. We are insatiable seekers of truth and have questions that demand answers. We know things here do not satisfy, but we continue to seek. C. S. Lewis said, "If we find ourselves with a desire that nothing in this world can satisfy, the most probable explanation is that we were made for another world" (Lewis C., 1952, p. 136).

The purpose of this book is to offer a new and refreshing method of analyzing the evidence for the existence of God. This era of scientific discovery has reanimated the Christian search for truth. With all the new scientific data regarding the beginning of the universe and the precision of laws of nature for the possibility of the existence of life, it is time for Christians to embrace the fact that God created everything and is revealing it to us. With the explosion of new information, we can be confident that it also concurs with the Bible.

Our God is a God of mercy, love, justice, and peace, but He is also creative and orderly and is a God of science, what used to be referred to as the philosophy of nature. General and special revelation are infallible, but our understanding and research of them is not. Science is not infallible; it is the study of nature. Just like science, theology is not infallible but is the study of God's special revelation.

Apologetics, the defense of the truth claims of Christianity, is basically a mechanism that boosts evangelism. It is the practice and skill of knowing worldviews and defending the Christian worldview against other belief systems. Admittedly, I am a neurologist and not a professional apologist or theologian. I enjoy studying medicine and apologetics, but I do not claim to have any great, new insights into the brilliant arguments that have been made through the last 2,000 years on the existence of the universe. But I hope to form new strategies to strengthen arguments that exist with new insights into medical discoveries that can relate to apologetics.

Neurology is a medical field dedicated to discovering the best explanation for a neurological problem a patient shows up ("presents" in medical lingo) with. This book is a blend of the ideas in neurological diagnostics with methods of Christian apologetics; I refer to this as medical apologetics. Since I have been studying apologetics, I have felt the need to find a way to weigh the evidence for God's existence.

In medicine, we systematize everything to help determine causes of medical problems and determine the best way to remedy them. In apologetics, there are numerous observations (cosmology, design, morality, consciousness, etc.) with so much information, so my goal is to develop methods to organize the evidence and weigh it using medical diagnostic tools.

In medicine, we use the cumulative weight of the evidence to make a diagnosis. When a physician has a strong suspicion of the cause of a disorder but a lab test doesn't support it, he doesn't disregard his suspicion, but he doesn't base the final decision on that lab test; he tries to find out in light of all of the other evidence what's going on.

We will use four medical techniques to deliberate and weigh the information for God's existence. First, we will use the neurological exam to "localize" the best explanation given the evidence. Second, we will utilize the multiple sclerosis (MS) diagnostic criteria that have a high level of diagnostic accuracy to determine the most likely explanation. Third, we will subject the observations and evidence to a special study to determine if there is an association between the observations and a Creator. And finally, we will determine whether that association is causally related, that is, if the effect following the supposed cause was indeed the result of that cause.

Christ Alone

Before we get into the good stuff, let me give some background on the importance of apologetics for me. Prior to coming to Christ around age twenty-two, I was struggling with this world and what it was offering me (and what I was offering it). The self-gratifying lifestyle I was drowning in hadn't satisfied my thirst for whatever it was I was seeking. I didn't know the answers, but I didn't have the right questions. More important, this world had not produced in me the solid personal character I longed for. I had abandoned morals and focused on immediate gratification through what I could easily see.

Though I had been exposed to Christianity through Catholicism growing up, I was actually very resistant to the Christian faith. It was not about my denial of God; it was about Christians. Something about them I just didn't like, but something about them made me envious. My perception was that they were sinless, untroubled, carefree, and naïve do-gooders, and I wasn't attracted to that lifestyle. I believed they were gullible and they didn't have struggles. I didn't like the idea of being accountable to anyone; I enjoyed my selfish choices. I was troubled, but I liked being troubled. I felt a sense of pride in the troubles I experienced (though most were self-inflicted). I did not realize that there was any depth to Christianity. I knew nothing of worldviews, moral arguments, or the value of human beings. I treated people as if they were just commodities able to provide me with things I needed. I had no virtue or sense of charity.

However, I believed in God though I didn't know anything about Him. I remember my pain and difficulties associated with drinking alcohol and would cry out to God with anger that He would allow me to suffer and not take it from me. Dark, lonely days filled with self-absorption and alcohol-induced decisions were going to kill me.

I had a conversation with a friend who was well aware of my struggles but decided to stick with me during them. He had given his life to Christ several years prior, and he knew all too well about the unsatisfying options this world offers. I looked up to him and respected his decision to follow Christ. However, I still wasn't sure Christianity (as I understood it) was something I wanted. I took pride in intellectualism and demonstrating how smart I was. During some of the Bible studies I attended with him, I'd act as if I were smarter than everyone else. For example, I read the entire Bible from start to finish in a couple of weeks to show everyone that I could do it and that I must have ended up with some biblical knowledge. It obviously doesn't work that way because I still had trouble understanding what the Bible was about. I was more focused on looking a certain way (intellectual) than accepting the truth of certain claims.

God Is Good

Coincidently during this time, because of my ongoing battles with addictions, I became very interested in the biological aspects of disease and addiction. I enjoyed studying the working of the nervous system, but I had not planned to pursue a career in it. I still had no direction but did not realize that.

One conversation with my friend helped satisfy some of my concerns about the Christian faith. We were in a sushi restaurant discussing some of the uneasiness I had about the Bible being a historical and accurate text. He was patient and gracious with me and answered my questions about archeology and geology. He opened my head to the possibility that Christianity might be true. He made me realize that just because I wasn't fond of my perspective on the few Christians I had met and judged to be naïve; my view of them was superficial. The character of the person who holds a belief has nothing to do with the truth of the belief itself. He recommended Lee Strobel's book *The Case for Christ*, which I quickly devoured. This began my quest for the truth of Christianity and my eventual submission to Christ as my Savior, and it changed the direction of my life ever since. This book is full of reasons to believe in God, but no one can deny the following evidence.

I had been a selfish, lying, deceitful thief on death's doorstep before Christ, but I have been transformed. Nothing else can explain that transition.

PART I

MEDICAL APOLOGETICS

CHAPTER 1

Neurologists and Apologists

Courage is almost a contradiction in terms. It means a strong desire to live taking the form of a readiness to die.

— *(Chesterton, Orthodoxy, 1908)*

Why Neurology?

Doctors are frequently asked why they decided to go into the specific field of medicine they chose. I chose neurology because of the complexity and order of the nervous system. The brain is bizarre and mystifying, and I was attracted to that. I did not choose neurology until my second year of medical school.

After four years of medical school and four more years of neurology residency training, I finally became a board-certified neurologist. Neurology continues to be the field of medicine with the most mystery. It is referred to as the final frontier of the human body. The more we study the nervous system, the more we find out how much we don't know. Paradoxes abound in the study of the human body, and the nervous system dominates in that regard. For example, the more we use the nervous system, the better is seems to get, yet with every other organ system, the opposite is true; overuse of them can actually result in damage (examples are problems with knees and osteoarthritis). If a person suffers an injury to the nervous system, by leaving it alone, the symptoms will worsen, not improve. If a person suffers a stroke and decides not to have physical therapy to maintain strength and range of motion of the affected limb, it will atrophy and become contracted and eventually lose all function. But with passive movement of the limb, it will slowly restore some of its function, and the brain can learn new pathways through neuroplasticity, its ability to adapt to new circumstances.

Why Apologetics?

Apologetics has changed my life and my understanding of the Christian faith; it continues to transform me. Apologetics has fostered in me a desire to avidly seek God's face. To know He is knowable is amazing and something that motivates me daily. To me, the study of the nervous system seems to yield results similar to those of the study of the divine. The breadth and depth of both fill me with wonder and offer me satisfaction in my searching and a hunger for more knowledge. Neurology continues to be a specialty in medicine that is often looked upon as intimidating. In the "bible" of neurology, *Principles of Neurology*, authors Adams and Victor state,

> Neurology is regarded by many as the most difficult and exacting medical specialty. Students and residents coming to the neurology ward or clinic for the first time are easily discouraged by what they see and are somewhat intimidated by the complexity of the nervous system. (Victor, 2001, p. 3)

Apologetics has a very similar feel to many Christians and has been considered more for the intellectual Christian. This has left apologetics to be somewhat untried and unstudied by many people. But we should not be intimidated by our faith; we should be encouraged we can learn about God. Christianity is not a blind faith though that is how secular culture describes it. The Bible says we are knowledge seekers and should seek to be wise. We are to use our minds and know why we believe what we do.

Knowing What You Believe

Apologetics can be a very useful means to understand and differentiate worldviews. Why do things work the way they do? Christian apologetics has been essential in my biblical understanding of this world and the people in it.

When I first came to Christ, like most people, I had questions. Many questions. Some important questions, but mostly questions for which I had been searching for answers for several years. At that time, I was studying biochemistry and molecular biology in college. I was always interested in how things worked. I had not yet decided on a career in medicine, but the functions in the cell intrigued me. The functions of proteins and amino acids especially drew my attention, and the explanations given by scientists as to why and how they developed were interesting as well.

It seemed to me that most of the development was assumed to have come about by random mutations and natural selection. This explanation did not satisfy me. I wondered (and continue to wonder) how these entities came to be in the first place and how the enzymatic processes seem to work on their own. The biochemical naturalistic explanation is based on gene mutations with natural selection weeding out the maladaptive mutations but keeping the adaptive ones. It boldly claims that given the random chance of genetic mutations with natural selection and genetic drift playing a role, we have life! And over a long amount of time, this has resulted in the complex processes in the cell that we see today. Really? That is a leap.

Medicine and Apologetics

As in biology, the field of medicine is full of mysteries and unknowns. The search for answers continues, but the number of questions grows. In medicine, we use empirical data and inference to choose treatment options. God has given us the ability to explore His creation and use it for good. He has disclosed Himself by general revelation through the creation of the universe and human consciousness. Humans are uniquely capable of studying our Creator and the rest of His creation.

The role of apologetics in my life has been extremely influential, and my hunger for answers to questions has been insatiable. I ponder matters from the origins of time and the universe to the structure and function of enzymes and DNA. My education in biology, chemistry, and physics built in me a foundational understanding of the basics of the complexities of life. Organic chemistry, physical chemistry, and molecular biology are my basics for understanding the inner workings of the cell. How do nerve cells function? The study of medicine has amplified this foundation from a biochemical standpoint to a deeper realm of advanced understanding and application of this science. How do medications affect dysfunctional neurons? Why do impaired cells cause disease?

My work in neurophysiology and clinical diagnostics is grounded in the care of the patient as a person seeking help and guidance. How do I make certain neurological diagnoses, and more important, how does the diagnosis of a disease such as amyotrophic lateral sclerosis (Lou Gehrig's disease) affect the person and his or her family? The most common and difficult question patients ask me as a neurologist is, "How did I get this?" or "Why did I get this?" This question is filled with emotional undertones, and only the Christian worldview truly gives a comprehensive and hopeful answer to this question. This is similar to the difficult questions raised by apologetics such as, "What hope is there to offer a young child dying of a terminal illness?"

Just as medical training improves our ability to offer human beings the best available evidence-based explanations and treatment, the study of apologetics deepens our understanding of science, philosophy, theology, and history to offer this world the best explanations for reality and the ultimate hope that we have.

Apologetics in the Bible

Apologetics is not necessary for salvation or faith in Christ. However, Jesus told us we were to "make disciples of all nations." In 1 Peter 3:15, we are told to "always have an answer for everyone who asks for the reason for the hope that we have." In Colossians, Paul instructed us to know good philosophy. C. S. Lewis stated in a message after World War II, "Good philosophy must exist, if for no other reason, because bad philosophy needs to be answered." (Lewis C., The Weight of Glory, 1949, p. 58). Acts 17 is filled with different examples of the first Christian apologist, Paul, using arguments in Thessalonica and in Athens to "prove Christ." Jude 1:3 reads, "Dear friends, although I was eager to write you about the salvation we share, I found it necessary to write and exhort you to contend for the faith that was delivered to the saints once for all." Jude stated clearly that we were to contend, make an argument, and assert the faith. He also made it clear that faith was delivered once for all; it had already been delivered so there was no more to make of it.

We are confident that the Bible is complete and that the faith we have is solid and true. We are to be confident in this and contend for its truth. How do we go about contending for it? We need to give reasons for why we know it is true.

The Youth Exodus and De-Baptism

If not for our own satisfaction and search for the face of God, our motivation should be for our unbelieving friends, our youth, the next generation. Apologetics may not be the same for everyone, but we are all called to know why we believe what we believe. As a pluralistic society, we pick and choose the philosophies that fit our desires. In this day of pluralism and modernism, we need to engage with people who have views different from ours. Even more important is arming the next generation with the knowledge to combat bad philosophy when they go off to college. It is discouraging to see so many Christian young people leave the faith when they go to college and are exposed to new ideas that are forced on them as truth and fact when they had never heard of any of those arguments before. It is our duty to arm these young people with a faith grounded in confidence and truth.

According to a Barna survey, 70 to 75 percent of Christian youth walk away from their faith after high school (Kinnaman, 2011). The main reasons have to do with their exposure to new questions and doubts about their faith once they start college. In *What's So Great About Christianity*, Dinesh D'Souza states,

> Children spend the majority of their waking hours in
> school. Parents invest a good portion of their life savings

in college education and entrust their offspring to people who are supposed to educate them. Isn't it wonderful that educators have figured out a way to make parents the instruments of their own undoing? Isn't it brilliant that they have persuaded Christian moms and dads to finance the destruction of their own beliefs and values? Who said atheists aren't clever? (D'Souza, 2007)

These are powerful words that seem to ring true today. Using a medical analogy, it is similar to hypertension and the risk of stroke; it is a modifiable and controllable risk that can usually be improved and managed to prevent later injury to the heart and brain. As Christian parents, we need to arm our children with the knowledge and resources so they are not unprepared for this battle.

I am impressed with professors such as Sean McDowell at Biola University, who exposes his students to the arguments against the Bible and God to disclose this information to them before they end up in the battle later on their own. They meet with skeptics, atheists, and professors of other worldviews who do not share their reasons for what they believe. This is critical so they are not overwhelmed later in life when all the information is forced on them in intimidating and new environments. One of our duties is to equip the younger generation to withstand the pressures of academia in their battle to win the younger generation's minds. This is a huge problem in the church right now; Frank Turek has referred to it as the Youth Exodus Problem, and it is critical to turn this around.

People around the world are exposed to the hype of so-called reason rallies and de-baptism rituals. If you have been baptized as an infant "against your will," you are welcomed to be de-baptized and enlightened to "get your soul back." This is clearly a mockery of an ancient, sacred, religious, public act of humility. De-baptisms are meant to stir the pot of reason and renounce religion as a delusion. How are we to respond to these problems?

Spiritual Vacuum

You might be surprised by this, but atheists and agnostics are not to blame; we Christians have not prepared our youth for this onslaught. As we remove ourselves from a culture, we leave a spiritual vacuum, and the expectation should be that it will become filled by something. Without Christianity, it has been secularized. The good thing about this is that Christianity has answers that are better than naturalism's answers.

Intellectual Christianity has reemerged as a juggernaut in the realms of science and philosophy. Secular academics have won the hearts and minds of our young people, and it is our duty to engage in this battle. We need to reenter culture and learn how to occupy this world without becoming of the world. We are without excuses, but the options and resources are at our fingertips. Secular philosophers and academics have been slowly winning, but this is changing fast, and they know it. And we have our trust in the Lord. We know His church will never fail. He does not need us, but it is our duty as His ambassadors to be obedient to and follow Him.

The next generation needs us. The next generation seems to be very inquisitive and has many great questions and a lot of interest in morality. So what do we do? How do we engage? We must first look at the purpose of apologetics and its applications to culture. In their book *Restoring All Things*, John Stonestree and Warren Cole Smith give many incredible stories about the ways Christians are impacting culture and shaping the world (Stonestree, 2015). They talk about ways we can promote what is good and change what is not. There are many other great resources available, and it is our duty to take advantage of them.

The Roles of Apologetics

Apologetics is multifactorial. First, it is a focused method to introduce seekers to the knowability of the Christian God. It helps us answer difficult questions and equip the younger generation that will need to engage in a pluralistic culture that wants to win their minds.

Second, apologetics is essential to give us the perspective of how to deal with the current immediate cultural and moral crises while focusing on the ultimate outcome. It helps us shape culture into a form that is receptive to Christianity. In deeply secularized society, Christianity is misunderstood and appears foreign and undesirable. Apologetics builds a positive case for Christianity, and it helps defend against attacks.

Third, apologetics builds a defense for the truth of Christianity. The defense of Christianity was the main role that the early church fathers took on against the heretical ideas such as Arianism that were popping up.

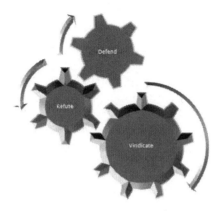

Figure 1. Gears working together as illustration
of the combined roles of apologetics.

Along with the defense of the gospel, a close companion role is the refutation of false beliefs. The purpose of apologetics is not to win arguments but to help people become open to the gospel message of Jesus Christ. Many people claim no one comes to Jesus through argument, but that's not the point. With all the scientific and historical evidence pointing to the God of the Bible, we can make the case for Christianity in a post-Christian world. This makes the cultural mind-set open to the possibility of an intellectual case for Christianity. The authority of academia has bulldozed Christianity out of classrooms and colleges. Without apologetics, the gospel message is not received as well as it could be. Apologetics works as a set of gears. The general roles of providing vindication and proofs move with the roles of refutation and defense.

As Christians, we know Jesus has overcome and will make all things new. Yet we live in a cultural climate of secularization and pluralism. How can we do so without accommodating to it? In *Mere Christianity*, C. S. Lewis states,

> If you read history you will find that the Christians who did the most for the present world were just those who thought most of the next ... It is since Christians have

largely ceased to think of the other world that they have become so ineffective in this (Lewis C., 1952, p. 134).

This world is hungry for information. In *Oh Brother Where Art Thou?* the gritty Hollywood "modern" remake of Homer's *Odyssey*, George Clooney plays a witty and garrulous con man who always has something to say but never has any answers. His character mentions several times throughout the movie, "Everyone's lookin' for answers." That may be true, but to find answers, we need to ask the right questions. Technology has blessed us with an unimaginable amount of data to search through for answers, but we need to know what the questions are. The millennial generation is exposed to such large amounts of information that it is not equipped to know what is good information and what is misinformation. It is encouraging to see so many apologists over the last few years battling to engage the next generation.

The arguments for the existence of God from cosmology and sufficient reason to teleology and the moral law are weighty and powerful. However, these are not subjects or topics normally included in church youth group curricula or taught in church service. With the explosion of information on the Internet, it has become a necessity to deliver this information in an accessible fashion.

Evangelism

Apologetics is an extension of evangelism that comes into play when the gospel is not necessarily good news to certain people. I had an encounter with a young man while I was working a midnight shift in the emergency room on one of my rotations. He was in a padded room because we were afraid he was suicidal. I had learned to be very gentle in these situations. I took my time to listen and build a rapport with him. He was clearly struggling and felt aimless in this life. He said, "I want to kill myself so all this pain and anxiety will go away." That was a critical point in the encounter. It is easy for physicians and caregivers to just disregard this and move on to the psychiatry referral and then on to the next patient. But in these situations, I experience compassion for these people and have a desire to help them. This is a battle for eternity. So the best thing is obviously not to say, "Yeah, but not today since I'm having you involuntarily committed until you're safe to be on your own." That doesn't help anyone. More helpful is to get into a discussion of the consequences of suicide for the person and the people they would leave behind.

This discussion led to a deeper contemplation of the impact of his decisions. He said he had never really considered the idea that a person may not go to heaven and why God would let someone into heaven. He had never really heard the gospel and did not realize he was valued highly in the Lord's sight. He had accepted the trite and misinformed notions that all religions were the same and that God wouldn't send anyone to hell; he had accepted this without ever knowing why. Most people tend to believe things because someone who has authority has said they are true.

Ignaz Semmelweis

We must know when and how to use apologetics. Even when others are certain they are right, we must always use gentleness and respect. It is important in all relationships to know how to offer the truth with grace. It does no good to force truth on others when they are satisfied with their beliefs. Without grace, we tend to cause defensiveness that results in a wall of pride in our opposition going up. Ultimately, forcing truth without grace could turn others away from it and harden their hearts toward receiving it again. That is why we must be winsome in this endeavor.

With the shouting and raucous militant atheism, this can be difficult, and our aim may be misdirected to trying to win every argument. But that is not the aim. Take a lesson from the story of Ignaz Semmelweis, an infamous Hungarian obstetrician. He graduated from Vienna medical school in 1844 and was accepted into an appointment to work in obstetrics (Nuland, 1988).

During this time, most pregnant mothers delivered their babies to midwives at home, but many others delivered in the hospital in Vienna. Semmelweis became interested in a quite common illness called childbed fever, or puerperal fever, which had an astounding mortality rate of 20 to 25 percent (Nuland, 1988). He discovered that the obstetrics ward in the Vienna hospital managed by the physicians and medical students had a childbed fever rate that resulted in as many as 800 deaths per year; another obstetrics ward in the hospital managed by midwives had a much lower rate of childbed fever that resulted in about 60 deaths per year.

After much research, he eventually concluded that the cause of childbed fever was contamination the doctors themselves were responsible for. Physicians and medical students would frequently go from pathological examination of cadavers to treating live patients, and hand-washing was not common practice at the time. This resulted in the transmission of cadaver material to the maternity ward. Semmelweis instituted the practice of rigorous hand-washing after cadaver examination, which resulted in the rate of puerperal fever dropping to only 1.2 percent (Nuland, 1988).

That is a great story, but it doesn't end there. Oddly, Semmelweis's finding did not please everyone; it basically meant the physicians and medical students were unknowingly responsible for many of these deaths by transmitting the infections. To make matters worse, Semmelweis had very poor abilities when it came to persuading his colleagues. In a biography of Semmelweis, Sherwin Nuland stated, "He was not averse to letting those who questioned him know that they must think of themselves as murderers if they did not wash their hands. He was a fire-spewing evangelist ... the kind of righteous goad that no one wants to be near" (Nuland, 1988, p. 250). People were put off by his manner of persuasion. Of note, the germ theory of infections had not yet been realized. But had he not been so belligerent in the way he communicated the evidence, many more physicians would have probably accepted his research and many fewer newborns would have paid the price. Semmelweis had the truth but no grace. When we have the truth, we are commanded to share it but with gentleness and respect. The consequences of doing otherwise can be devastating.

As a neurologist, I aim at understanding the complexity of the nervous system. The macroanatomy, cortical architecture, nerve physiology, and biochemistry are all separately staggering. The smallest effects have huge impacts. As a Christian, I consider the complexity of life, origin, suffering, meaning, purpose, fellowship, and worship to be staggering. My goal with this book is not to prove the existence of God; it is an attempt to give an explanation for the existence of a loving and powerful Creator who designed us as special in this humungous universe. The goal of this book is to glorify the one true God. This is a guide to a different understanding of the complexity of His creation. It is an attempt to understand the importance of each human and the majesty of his or her Creator. It is a realization that as we dig deeper into the mystery of Him, we will gain knowledge and wisdom and develop a sense of wonder and awe at how little we actually know. As the Lord said to Job,

> Who is this who obscures My counsel with ignorant words? Get ready to answer me like a man; when I question you, you will inform me. Where were you when I established the earth? Tell Me, if you have understanding. Who fixed its dimensions? Certainly you know! Who stretched a measuring line across it? What supports its foundations? Or who laid its cornerstone while the morning starts sang together and all the sons of God shouted for joy? ... Where is the road to the home of light? Do you know where darkness lives, so you can lead it back to its border? Don't you know? You were already born; you have lived so long! (Job 38:2–7, 19–21)

CHAPTER 2

Medicine and Theology

Do doctors believe in God? A 2005 study that asked 1,044 U.S.-trained physicians this question concluded that 76 percent believed in God and 59 percent believed in some sort of afterlife. Approximately 55 percent stated that their religious beliefs affected how they practiced (Curlin, 2005). This trend seems to continue in medicine as a 2015 survey by Medscape revealed that 75 to 77 percent of medical doctors consider themselves religious (Peckham, 2015). Researcher Dr. Farr Curlin at the University of Chicago's MacLean Center for Clinical Medical Ethics stated, "We were surprised to find that physicians were as religious as they apparently are." But why is this so surprising?

The Physician Compartment

Is there a disparity between medical doctors and scientists when it comes to belief in the supernatural? In The God Delusion, Richard Dawkins quotes a study that portrays most scientists as atheists. Physicians are placed in a unique realm or compartment wedged between the medical science of the laboratory and the application of that science in life-and-death situations with human beings. Physicians are on the front lines of disease and death if you will, whereas scientists are mostly in labs working on the deep scientific questions; they work with rodents, bacteria, or primates rather than with living, breathing humans.

Scientists don't make life-or-death decisions for treatments and management of an illness or disease. They don't have the advantage of seeing the nonphysical and spiritual reactions and experiences physicians encounter. A biologist studies the amazing and complex integration of the machinery inside the cell, but physicians apply the medical knowledge and therapeutic strategies to the person. They confront death and dying in real time and in real people and deal with the ramifications of their decisions.

Physicists study how quantum particles interact or how stars are formed but are not directly related to an experience with the struggle for life in the setting of disease. The physician, in the middle compartment, must reach down into the scientific compartment to grasp the knowledge and experience from basic medicine and biology and take it up to the clinical compartment for application to the person. When they apply their biological knowledge to human beings, it becomes more than just an academic exercise in knowledge and education. The examination and treatment of patients is transformed from basic science into a purposeful and relevant function that can provide therapy for other human beings.

The reason we medical doctors are more likely to believe in a supernatural creator is because we see things medical science cannot explain. We see tumors disappear. We see brains that are healed of MS lesions. We see people walk again after half of their brains had been destroyed by trauma. We see people come back from the grave. Obviously, some physicians become very cynical just as some in any profession do, but physicians generally see life as precious.

Medical doctors are in a unique position in relation to medical ethics, philosophy, religion, and science. Medical ethics takes center stage for the physician and the worldview that the physician holds; the way he or she sees the patient will often drive the proper ethical decisions.

Scientific Authority

I don't know of many neurologist apologists. Most physicians in general do not necessarily seem to be interested in investigating the deep questions of origin and morality. I am not saying this to criticize physicians but to make a point that physicians are taught to treat patients but along the way are forced to think certain things due to the enormous amount of information they have to grapple with.

I think that this is true for several reasons. First, physicians study and train for many years with a focus on finally being able to practice medicine on their own. During those long training years, they are taught the basic sciences in depth including cell biology, genetics, and chemistry. Evolution is interwoven in these subjects, and most make a lot of sense at the time.

We physicians are told, "Science doesn't have all the answers yet, but it will eventually." We believe our professors because they have inside science knowledge and a sense of authority; we must learn what we are taught.

We believe it when they tell us the reason for certain enzyme processes is due to natural selection acting on genetic mutations over time. We believe them when they say the reason for such "striking similarity" among the limb bones/structure between humans, horses, whales, and bats is due to a common ancestor (rather than a common creator). Most of us were never exposed to any alternative to these evolutionary ideas. We figured that since the professors were teaching us, we were there to learn the latest and most accurate science. They were the authority on the topic, right?

Well, maybe not. Contrary to what the media portrays, professors are not infallible. Impressionable pupils are ripe for the picking among the academic elite. In science fields, we need to think critically and not allow ourselves to be bound by the limitations of the materialists saying nature is all there is. The universe speaks to us, and we should listen. G. K. Chesterton stated, "The grass seemed signaling to me with all its fingers at once; the crowded stars seemed bent upon being understood" (Chesterton, Orthodoxy, 1908).

Second, physicians spend so much time studying volumes and loads of information to get through our studies and research in medical school training that even if we had the audacity to question evolution, we are not allotted the time to investigate the other side. It is interesting to note that even Charles Darwin pointed out the importance of having information from both sides of an argument: "A fair result can be obtained only by fully stating and balancing the facts and arguments on both sides of each question" (Darwin, 1859, pp. Introduction, p. 2).

In residency, we spend hundred-hour weeks in the hospital with patients to learn diagnosis and treatment while figuring out how to effectively manage sleep deficiency. Due to the intense nature of medical training and the relentless information flood, we are forced to accept what we are taught as fact. Most physicians probably believe in macroevolution not because they understand it or because they have a good grasp of any alternatives but mostly because that's what they have been taught. When physicians first see the evidence against macroevolution, they can be surprised. I think the same thing happens when we are finally open to seeing the depth of the truth of Christianity. When people are exposed to these truths, they realize they basically had not been exposed to the breadth of information and alternatives.

As a neurologist, I see the way people struggle to find answers to their questions, and it's difficult when there aren't many answers to offer them. Unlike neurology and medicine, Christianity has the answers to all the questions. It is the best answer to life's most challenging questions, and it offers more to make sense of the human predicament in this world than any other worldview. It is the most consistent and internally coherent belief system. We will spend time reviewing why that is the case in this book.

The Atheist's Misdiagnosis

Physicians train to become great diagnosticians and treaters. The art of diagnosis is based on fundamentals and experience. Diagnostics are learned through mastering different techniques and then learning how to use such techniques and the tools available to finalize a diagnosis. The methods of diagnosis in neurology come from the perspective of an elaborate and mysterious examination technique that investigates the body through testing the nervous system. This is a system of primary, secondary, and sometimes tertiary sets of skills to determine if there is a neurologic disorder and where the problem is in the nervous system. I believe this can be applied to more than just the patient in the exam room. People use diagnostic tools all the time. With experience, we all have come to examine and interpret the world in different ways, but we all come with biases. So we must examine the evidence in the best way without our philosophical biases. This is essential for correct diagnoses.

In residency training, we are often taught to begin fresh with every new patient and not read the volumes of prior medical records they often bring with them. If we read the prior records from other physicians, that would give us biases toward those physicians' thought processes and would affect our ability to base the encounter solely on our impressions as we meet the patient.

Atheists tend to begin all their encounters with the presupposition that God does not exist. No matter where the truth leads them, they often have already concluded it could not lead to God. William Lane Craig stated in his Reasonable Faith podcast that in a debate in Canada, the atheist he was arguing with stated, "Even if Jesus came down from Heaven right in front of me, I would still not bow my knee to Him!" This is what I call the atheist's misdiagnosis; atheists have misdiagnosed the cause of the cosmos. When a physician makes the wrong diagnosis, the consequences can be devastating to the patient. Those who knowingly deny the diagnosis disregard the reason they feel the way they do. Without the correct final diagnosis, the way they look at the treatment of how things are will be wrong. This is the same with the universe. There is a cause, and there is a reason things are the way they are. There is treatment and a cure, and it is crucial to get the diagnosis right.

Medicine Is Meant to Restore

God intended His creation to be perfect. As G. K. Chesterton stated, "God had written, not so much a poem, but rather a play; a play he had planned as perfect, but which had necessarily been left to human actors and stage-managers, who had since made a great mess of it" (Chesterton, Orthodoxy, 1908, p. 71). Because of the Fall and the consequent entrance of sin into this creation, there is disease, despair, and death. Disease tends to be the cause of death. This was not the way God intended the world to be. As humans, we have chosen to do things our way rather than God's way, and that has resulted in a disruption of the created order.

Physicians are blessed with the opportunity and the challenge to try to restore some of the damaging effects of the Fall. With the general revelation of God and the technology He has given us, we can offer treatments for many illnesses and disorders. Through the gifts of the Holy Spirit, we can reverse some of the diseases in this world and help restore some of the natural, perfect order He intended. As a doctor, it is my daily privilege to do this for Him. It is not always that easy, and the human body is incomprehensibly complicated (hence the intense and prolonged medical training).

Weighing the Evidence

The practice of medicine has only recently in the last half century become extensively evidenced-based. The traditional practice using good medical judgment based on knowledge and experience has been usurped by the explosion of results from clinical studies and research trials. Empiric treatment based on medical literature has revolutionized the health care standard in America. Physicians are trained to examine the evidence and build a case for a diagnosis and treatment plan. Throughout their medical training, they learn the medical foundations and methods for designing research and interpreting its results.

Just because there is literature on a certain topic does not mean it is worthwhile or even credible. There is good data and bad data, and it can be difficult to weed through some of the worthwhile data. Just as on the Internet, many things are published that are often just not true. It is the job of the good physician to determine what's reliable data and good medicine or not. We physicians are trained to weigh the evidence and apply it to the current patient's situation. For example, in the treatment of acute stroke, the American Stroke Association recommendation for administration of the "clot-buster" tpa (tissue plasminogen activator) is within three and four and a half hours of the onset of stroke symptoms. However, scenarios arise in which this window of treatment needs to be broken or bent. If a thirty-year-old man presents with a large left middle cerebral artery stroke that started five hours earlier and he has lost all language capabilities and movement of the right side of his body, the risk of giving the medication beyond four and a half hours needs to be weighed against not doing anything. The chances of him ending up with a lifelong devastating neurological injury may outweigh the risk of giving the medicine too late. Most neurologists would choose to offer that medication to him.

Can We Know Anything?

We must be careful with the idea of empirical treatment and knowledge. Currently, society wants evidence for everything. But what does that mean? Empiricism is the idea that we have to observe something to know anything about it. But there are plenty of things we know that exist though we haven't observed them. For example, atoms and electrons are observed through indirect methods of testing but not directly by any of the five senses. Contrary to popular belief, the source of knowledge therefore does not have to rely solely on the five senses. It is important to understand where knowledge comes from and what the different kinds of knowledge are. From scripture, we understand that knowledge is a gift from God. Knowledge and wisdom come from God's Word (Proverbs 2:6). Knowledge of God is valuable; knowledge without God is chasing the wind. Knowledge for its own sake puffs up and makes one proud (1 Corinthians 13:2).

There are typically three types of knowledge—propositional, knowledge by acquaintance, and skill knowledge or know-how. Propositional knowledge is the knowledge of facts such as those we get out of textbooks or historical information. It may inform us of what was going on during the Revolutionary War, but Paul Revere had firsthand knowledge since he was present then.

Christianity uses all three sources of knowledge to make sense of things. Unfortunately, many people know a lot about scripture and biblical history but don't know God. They have a propositional knowledge but no knowledge by acquaintance. Moreover, some may say the Lord does not require knowledge of know-how as a Christian. That may be a half-truth. Salvation does not require works, but we are commanded to know what we believe and strengthen our faith. It is recommended that we seek truth and the face of God. Proverbs 18:15 says, "The mind of the discerning acquires knowledge, and the ear of the wise seeks it."

To Vaccinate or Not

We must seek knowledge and understanding in this generation of uber-information. An example of bad published data in the medical literature that has caused harm and controversies has to deal with vaccinations related to autism (Wakefield, 1998). This connection between vaccination and autism created a cultural uproar that continues today despite the fact that the article was removed from the journal due to fraudulent data it contained. Countless online medical journals publish poorly designed studies and anecdotal cases. It is important to know how to find good data, how to interpret it well without requiring the statistical gymnastics so many researchers perform to get their results, and then how to apply it to patients.

Complexity and Order

We need to use good judgment in medicine because there is much we do not know. We neurologists use several tools to help determine whether something is caused by a problem with the nervous system. The complexity of the nervous system cannot be ignored, and we can examine it only with wonder and awe. Though it is complex, it does not mean there is no order or that we cannot see the design and structure of the nervous system.

As a Christian, I am intrigued by the Creator. The complexity of the Lord is amazing. I love paradoxes, and the study of God is the greatest paradox. As Charles Spurgeon so eloquently stated, "Study of the divine is both awe-inspiring and humbling at the same time," (Spurgeon, 1855). The great paradoxes of the Christian religion are unique and unavoidable. The more we learn about God, the more humbled we are by His majesty. This seems to be true also for the foundation of the universe as we know it. Brilliant thinkers from ancient times including Aristotle to recent physicists such as Stephen Hawking attempt to answer the most basic questions of all time: why is there something rather than nothing? Where did the laws of nature come from? The more we examine the evidence and clues to these questions, the more questions we have.

For example, when evolutionary theory was constructed, the complexity of cell biology was unknown. This is what biologist Michael Behe calls Darwin's black box. Electron microscopy had not yet demonstrated the micromachinery in the cell for biologists in Darwin's time to witness. The specificity and information that cell biology revealed generated an explosion of new answers and questions regarding the origin of everything.

As a specialist in the nervous system, I don't consider this a trivial matter. The importance of the complexity of the body overall is humbling.

Physicians Can't Be Atheists

Why are physicians to treat the human body with such respect and the person with such dignity? If it is true as atheists testify that we are just machines made up of biochemistry resulting in behaviors (either advantageous or not), it should not matter how physicians treat patients. This is not how the world works; this is contrary to the history of medicine and humanity.

Why do we treat diseases and try to find cures if life is just about propagating genetic information to offspring? Physicians do not sweep this question under the rug; they focus on each person. They care about each other as human beings. They treat persons rather than diseases. As a specialist in the inflammatory neurodegenerative disorder, multiple sclerosis, I and my patients understand this.

DNA Does Not Explain Everything

I have spent a decade studying the nervous system from the biochemical basics of neurotransmitter production and metabolism to the clinical manifestations of neurologic problems. The more that we look into the cell, the more we see the complexity of life and evidence of specific purpose. As we look and study, the more we realize it is not explained by unguided changes. Genetics is not simple; since the discovery of DNA and the mapping of the genetic code in the 1990s, we seem to have an even harder time than before explaining problems.

Let's take a brief look at some of the genetics involved in the development of disease. We know that just because certain people have genetic mutations, they will not necessarily manifest the disease that may be related to those mutations; DNA does not equal disease. Studies of identical twins reveal this. For example, if one identical twin has multiple sclerosis, the chances that the other will get MS even with the same DNA is not 100 percent. It is not even 50 percent. It's only about 30 percent. This means that twin has a good chance of *not* developing MS even though the other identical twin has developed it and they were probably raised in the same environment. Furthermore, every person with MS seems to have a different course of the disease.

Another example involves genetics in Alzheimer's disease. Several genetic mutations can result in the development of this common cause of dementia. If a person has a certain mutation of a gene (mutated homozygosity of one of the apolipoprotein E epsilon alleles), he or she has a higher chance of developing Alzheimer's. This gene is present on chromosome 19 and exists in three locations on each chromosome. We all have two copies of this gene. However, it is not medically recommended to check for this mutation since most people who have it do not go on to develop Alzheimer's. That's because DNA problems alone are not sufficient to cause dementia and therefore don't equate with the development of diseases. So just because a person has this allele doesn't mean he or she will acquire Alzheimer's. The presence of one copy of the allele increases the risk about two- or threefold, and having both copies of the allele increases the risk to eight- to twelvefold, but it does not guarantee the disease.

The risk goes from about one in seven to about one in three after age eighty. The genetics do not completely predict the outcome (Corbo, 1999). This is important to understand especially in this modern era of atheistic explanation of everything from evolution. DNA does not explain everything. Evolution does not explain everything. There are better explanations. Human beings are not just biochemistry and behavior.

Medication Response

To illustrate the complexity of a single disease further, let's consider some more about the spectrum of a disorder such as MS. Many medications for it are available, but not everyone responds the same to each medication. There is currently no way of knowing which MS patient will respond to this or that medication. All the medications for multiple sclerosis have an effect on the immune system, but many people do not benefit from some of the medications. They each work a little differently, and each person responds differently.

Besides the impact of inflammation in the nervous system in MS, the effects on the rest of the body are substantial including muscle function and urinary and gastrointestinal problems. The complexity of system involvement is astounding and can be quite challenging in terms of treatment.

The amount of research on the immune system's involvement in MS has been profound, and there is significant evidence that even the bacteria in the gut probably play a role in the development and course of MS. (We'll discuss this in a later chapter.)

Diet seems to be a factor in the development of the type of bacteria in the GI system. These bacteria talk in a sense to our immune systems. The different cells of the immune system (T cells and B cells) regulate inflammatory response versus protection of the nervous system.

Parkinson's Disease in Worms

The mystery and majesty of the brain is humbling. There is usually no simple answer in clinical neurology. From memory and cognition to language production and speech, to sensation and perception and motor planning to locomotion, the complexity and specificity of the nervous system is beyond the ability of unguided processes to produce over a finite period. Evolution is not a good explanation for the development of the nervous system of a worm let alone of a human.

We can cause Parkinson's disease in worms by manipulating their nervous systems, but we cannot figure out the mechanisms that cause it in humans. By disrupting the dopamine pathway through genetic modifications in the nematode roundworm *Caenorhabditis elegans*, a worm form of Parkinson's disease is produced that impairs movement similar to loss of normal movement in human Parkinson's disease (Harrington, 2010). But it is not as simple as that in humans, and it is clearly not ethical to perform these studies on human beings.

As I pointed out earlier, physicians do not live out atheism. If atheism were true, physicians wouldn't need to treat terminal diseases. Antibiotics for sinus and bladder infections are fine, but why would we treat a terminal illness? According to atheism, it shouldn't matter because there is nothing special about humans. Our nervous system may be more complex than that of an earthworm, but humans are just more-complicated animals down the evolutionary tree from them. This is harsh, but according to atheism, it wouldn't be advantageous to the human species for people with terminal diseases to exist. Naturalism doesn't offer hope. Without hope, nothing has meaning.

Furthermore, evolution doesn't explain why physicians treat patients as more than just their bodies. We treat them as fellow human beings who are complex. We treat them as we would want to be treated. The history of medicine has never recommended dispensing of a damaged human as we would a broken piece of equipment even if it weren't fixable.

Neurology has classically been the field of medicine with the most "incurable" disorders, but neurologists don't discard people as we would inexpensive watches that stopped working. We treat them as fellow human beings with intrinsic worth and value. Why? If we were truly to live out atheistic beliefs, we wouldn't do that. It wouldn't be useful to civilization to keep certain people alive if we all lived out atheism. The implications of human beings living by atheistic standards doesn't equate to free thinking and freedom but to dehumanization and the exclusion of supposedly weaker human beings.

Christianity is the only worldview that embraces all humanity. God uses the weakest and poorest to bring about His glory in this universe. The ultimate being gave up His throne to come and be among us and feel the same things we feel and suffer. He understands what we go through. This "person" created all and sustains all. There is no evidence for the nonexistence of this person. Naturalism tries to deny a creating and sustaining being but does nothing to explain why things are the way they are. The case for the Christian faith is overwhelming. Let's review it in the context of a diagnosis. Let's weigh the evidence of the available options to come up with the best explanation for why things are the way they are.

Christianity Offers a Cure

The realm of apologetics is not new; it has been around for at least two millennia. In Acts 17, Paul defended the faith. St. Augustine of Hippo defended the faith against heresies such as Arianism. Thomas Aquinas built arguments for the "proof" of God. But in an age of new ideas and new discoveries, faith is an ever-changing realm. As science deepens our understanding of cell biology and genetics, archeology reinforces the authority of the Bible and history teaches us the truth of Christianity. We are thus encouraged and emboldened to preach the gospel of Christ and defend the faith.

I am privileged to take part in the care of such strong patients. A neurological diagnosis can be devastating for patients and their families; I see the impact of these diagnoses but also see the courage and the strength these people have. Where does that come from? Often from their faith. Faith in Christ acts as a psychological crutch for hurting people, but it is the medicine and the cure as well. Religion is portrayed negatively by atheists as being a crutch for weak people. That's fine. That's the point. We all need that help. However, it is wrong to call religion but not atheism a crutch. As Julian Huxley stated, "The sense of spiritual relief which comes from rejecting the idea of God as a supernatural being is enormous," (Huxley, 1964, p. 223). He meant that without that rejection of God, he would not have the relief of guilt and accountability to someone. He seems to use the idea of rejecting God as his crutch. Unlike Christianity, however, there is no medicine and there is no cure.

CHAPTER 3

Mysteries and Neurons

Pray also for me, that the message may be given to me when I open my mouth to make known with boldness the mystery of the gospel. For this I am an ambassador in chains. Pray that I might be bold enough in Him to speak as I should.

—Ephesians 6:19–20

The divine mysteries of existence and life can humble the mind. The way everything is so dependent on everything else inspires any person who takes the time to indulge in this phenomenon. On the biological level, neurons do not act alone. There is no known single-celled organism made up of a neuron; they are specialized pieces of machinery that act in unison. This mystery of the connection of human life with something beyond is easy to be aware of but difficult to fully grasp. G. K. Chesterton always said it well. In his poem "The Wise Men," Chesterton, the king of paradox displays his wit. The blessings of wisdom, yet the wisdom to know that we know not. Chesterton paints the picture of a simple way in his poem "The Wise Men" that is so easy to see, but we think we know so much that the way is actually too simple for us.

Step softly, under snow or rain,
    To find the place where men can pray;
The way is all so very plain
    That we may lose the way.
We know all labyrinthine lore,
    We are the three wise men of yore,
And we know all things but the truth.

Is Christianity Too Simple?

Chesterton stated, "It is not that the Christian ideal has been tried and found wanting. It is that Christianity has been found difficult and left untried." (Chesterton, What's Wrong with the World, 1910). In Luke 14, Jesus explained the cost of discipleship and the difficulty of following Him. We think we know so much. Malcolm Muggeridge said,

> Thus did Western Man decide to abolish himself, creating his own boredom out of his own affluence, his own vulnerability out of his own strength, his own impotence out of his own erotomania, himself blowing the trumpet that brought the walls of his own city tumbling down, and having convinced himself that he was too numerous, labored with pill and scalpel and syringe to make himself fewer. Until at last, having educated himself into imbecility, and polluted and drugged himself into stupefaction, he keeled over—a weary, battered old brontosaurus—and became extinct. (Barlow, 1985)

We seem to have an explanation for everything, yet the Lord proclaimed in Isaiah 55:8–9, "For My thoughts are not your thoughts, and your ways are not My ways. This is the LORD's declaration. For as heaven is higher than earth, so My ways are higher than your ways, and My thoughts than your thoughts."

Neurology and the Mystery of God

Neurology is a field full of mystery. In medical school, there continues to be a phenomenon referred to as neurophobia, a fear of neurological disorders due to how scary they look clinically. Trying to figure out a neurological problem intimidates many physicians. (This is unfortunately thought to be one of the reasons many medical students avoid going into neurology.)

The complexity and mystery of the nervous system can be a hindrance, but it's exactly what pulled me into the field. The configuration and the function of nerves fascinated me. The ability to systematically localize a neurological condition without ever having to order a lab test was intriguing to me. I wanted to be able to think through a patient's symptoms and use my clinical skills to build a case for a diagnosis, so I committed myself to understanding the nervous system through medical school and residency training.

I've discovered that the mystery of God is similar. Using clinical skills to localize the original source of the symptoms is like building a case for the best explanation using the available evidence. Neurologists use diagnostic exam skills and experience to explain problems. Apologists use examination skills and experience to explain the problems of the world. Why do we give so much weight to a probable neurological diagnosis even though there is no hundred-percent certainty? Why do we not give such weight to the existence of God as the source origin when there is so much certainty?

Our God Is Knowable

The study of the divine is the most satisfying of all intellectual pursuits. It expands our brains' capabilities and deepens our understanding. It humbles our minds and softens our hearts. The magnitude of wonder experienced in just thinking about the idea of God can be overwhelming. This has been expressed over the ages in numerous ways by many brilliant people. Charles Spurgeon put it this way.

There is something exceedingly improving to the mind in a contemplation of the Divinity. It is a subject so vast, that all our thoughts are lost in its immensity; so deep, that our pride is drowned in its infinity. Other subjects we can compass and grapple with; in them we feel a kind of self-content, and go our way with the thought, "Behold I am wise." But when we come to this master-science, finding that our plumb-line cannot sound its depth, and our eagle eye cannot see its height, we turn away with the thought that vain man would be wise, but he is like a wild donkey's colt; and with solemn exclamation, "I am but of yesterday, and know nothing. No subject will tend more to humble the mind, than the thoughts of God … But while the subject humbles the mind, it also expands it. He who often thinks of God, will have a larger mind than the man who simply plods around this narrow globe … The most excellent study for expanding the soul is the science of Christ, and him crucified, and the knowledge of the Godhead in the glorious Trinity. Nothing will so enlarge the intellect, nothing so magnify the whole soul of man, as a devout, earnest, continued investigation of the great subject of the Deity." (Spurgeon, 1855).

We are to seek God's face and acquire knowledge. Proverbs 18:15 says, "The mind of the wise acquires knowledge." We are encouraged to expand our minds by studying the divine. Unlike many other religious deities, our God is knowable.

A Neurology Primer

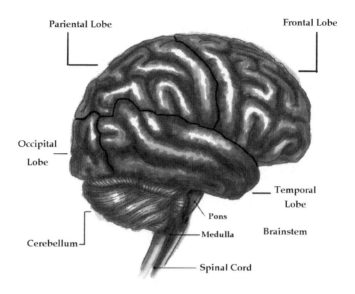

To understand some of the basics of the nervous system and the discussion in this book, let's review some of the anatomy and functions of the nervous system.

Neurology is the field of medicine that deals with the diagnosis and treatment of disorders of the nervous system. A simple way to picture the nervous system is to divide it into the central nervous system (the brain and spinal cord) and the peripheral nervous system (all the nerves in the rest of the body including the face, abdomen, and limbs). That's a major oversimplification, but it helps give a top-down overview to grasp the larger picture.

The brain is divided into many sections. Simply put, there are two hemispheres (left and right), and each hemisphere is divided into four lobes (frontal, parietal, temporal, and occipital). Each lobe is organized and has its main functions. The frontal lobe provides neurons involved in decision making, limb movement, and judgment, whereas the occipital lobe's main function involves perceiving and processing visual stimuli. The outside layer of the brain is called the cortex, and the underlying region of the brain is called the sub-cortex, the white matter. The cortex is a thin region made up mostly of neuron cells as well as other supporting cells. However, the cortex is not a simple, single layer of cells. In most parts of the brain, it's made up of six layers designated as layers I to VI. Each has a prime input and output from and to the regions of the brain and body it communicates with.

Different areas of the brain such as the primary motor cortex in the posterior frontal lobe have extensive and large neurons called pyramidal cells in layer V. These neurons are so big and important that we can pick up their electrical signals on an electroencephalogram (EEG). The cortex varies in thickness but averages about one to three millimeters. This changes with time and with certain disorders such as Alzheimer's.

Stars and Nerves

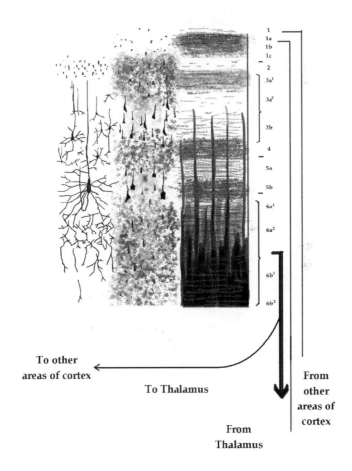

Please allow me to dive deeper into the importance of this structural design. The cortex is well organized for its particular region and function.

The nerve cells that make up the cortex connect with other neurons in it or send their extensions—axons—to other regions in the white matter and other deep-brain structures. The nerves connect with and communicate with other cells throughout the brain by synapses, connections between two nerves or a nerve and another cell (such as supporting brain cell, gland, muscle, etc.).

Synapses are the undergirding of brain function; they make the brain work properly. Properly functioning synapses allow memories to be formed and then retrieved and decoded. An important note to remember (form a new synapse here) is that the synapses are dynamic, not static; they can change and improve or deteriorate.

To illustrate the magnitude of these connections, think of the known universe. About 1 trillion galaxies are in the observable universe, and each galaxy has about 100 billion stars. Imagine this—there are about the same number of stars in the universe as there are synapses in the brain! This is barely fathomable.

Each of these synapses is regulated and controlled by enzymatic processes and neurotransmission of proteins and elements. The nerves don't come into contact with each other, but they talk across the synapses with language in the form of neurotransmitters.

Most people are familiar with some of the names of the brain's neurotransmitters such as dopamine and adrenaline (epinephrine). But there are many more, and they each have roles depending on which neuron sends it out and which neuron receives it. For example, there are at least four big dopamine pathways in the brain. One, the nigrostriatal pathway, is made up of neurons in a region of the brain called the substantia nigra near the top of the spinal cord. These neurons produce dopamine from the amino acid tyrosine in a fascinating enzyme pathway. These neurons are specialized and send signals and dopamine to the brain especially to the basal ganglia, the control center for our ability to plan and carry out movement.

Neurons in the cortex send signals to the basal ganglia to initiate or plan movements. Disruption to the nerves in the nigro-striatal system results in abnormal movement. This is the general problem in Parkinson's disease. The basal ganglia has neurons that beat so to speak in a regular frequency and deliver dopamine or inhibitory neurotransmitters to regulate the rhythm of the basal ganglia. With any disruption in the rhythm, abnormal clinical movements occur; these include what we see in patients with Parkinson's or who have tremors, abnormal limb postures, and other problems.

PARKINSON'S DISEASE

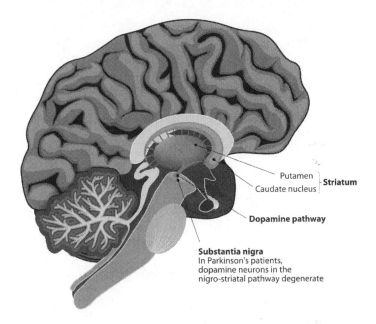

Putamen
Caudate nucleus } **Striatum**

Dopamine pathway

Substantia nigra
In Parkinson's patients,
dopamine neurons in the
nigro-striatal pathway degenerate

As you can see from just this example in which we went from a big-picture view at the level of the cortex down to the level of neurotransmission, the brain is complex and very specialized. This complexity and specialization extends through the brain into the spinal cord and out to the organs and body tissues. It results in an amazing ability to perceive and respond to environmental cues by sending and receiving messages. This is very important because it is how neurologists can localize—figure out where a problem is coming from. Understanding normal neuroanatomy and function is critical for determining whether a patient's symptoms are due to a nervous system problem or from a problem that comes from elsewhere.

Localizing the Lesion

We'll be using the localizing technique for diagnostics with other methods to weigh the evidence for the existence of God. We will introduce the approach of neurological localization in this chapter and apply it later.

The nervous system's organization allows us to localize where a problem is coming from. Neurologists are trained for four years during residency to become expert neurological examiners. The training is exhaustive and intended to act as the primary means of teaching diagnosis of a neurological disease.

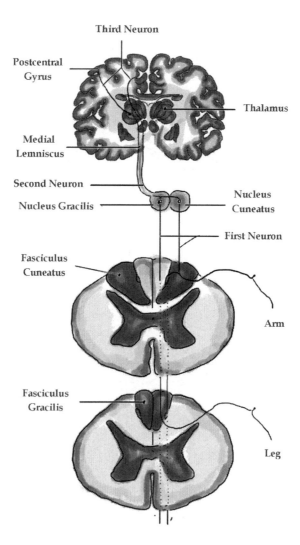

The nervous system can be divided into approximately seven localizing regions that include muscles, the neuromuscular junction, peripheral nerves, spinal nerve roots, spinal cord, brain stem, and the brain. These are subdivided more once the general source is discovered. For example, if a forty-year-old woman presents with a sudden onset of speech changes and left-arm weakness, the paramedic and emergency room physician are trained to think of the most serious and critical problem; in this case, they would likely think of a stroke as the cause.

Paramedics and emergency room providers do not have the luxury of several years of dedicated focus and training on the nervous system's anatomy and function. In the ER, the patient would likely get brain imaging with a CT scan or MRI and the neurologist on call would be consulted for possible stroke. However, the neurologist would not necessarily just be thinking of stroke in this patient because there are other reasons for her symptoms that may be even more likely than a stroke. The astute neurologist would be wondering why the patient has left-arm weakness and speech problems. This raises suspicion of something other than stroke because most people are right handed and if they had a left-brain stroke, that would affect language and the right arm, not the left.

The neurologist would have probably asked the ER physician several other questions about the patient such as the onset of symptoms and other risk factors for stroke and other explanations. The case is being built before even seeing the patient. The differential diagnosis is being formulated. By the time the neurologist sees the patient to draw more historical information and perform a neurological exam, there is often a main idea he or she will focus on. For instance, the patient may state that she had developed a severe, pounding headache with nausea and then over the course of about twenty or thirty minutes, her left hand became numb, and the numbness crept up her arm to her shoulder and neck.

The case for the best explanation is changing in the neurologist's mind. The patient is an otherwise healthy female with no risk factors for stroke. Her speech is slurred, but her language function is normal. Her vision is normal. She is able to move all limbs. Her left arm feels weak to her, but she is able to show some strength in it and has normal fine-motor control in her left hand.

The neurologist tests her deep-tendon reflexes and finds they are normal and similar to the right side of the body. The neurologist's fear of a stroke lessens. The best explanation based on all the evidence is a benign but no less frightening process associated with a type of migraine that can produce symptoms very similar to a stroke. The history and neurological exam do not localize to a vascular region of the brain, and so a stroke is less likely an explanation. The patient could undergo a brain MRI to more definitively rule out stroke and other processes and confirm the migraine diagnosis (and prove the intelligent neurologist right).

Hope but No Cure

There are often no cures for neurological diseases. For example, amyotrophic lateral sclerosis (ALS, Lou Gehrig's disease) is a devastating disease with no cure. The course is progressive; a person will live usually about three years from the onset of the disease. It is a fast, relentless accumulation of disability with loss of the ability to move, eat, and eventually breathe.

Parkinson's disease is another disorder that has no cure; nothing stops the disease from progressing. Dementia, Huntington's disease, and MS are progressive and severely disabling, and all are without medical cures. But that does not mean there is no treatment.

Over the past twenty years, there has been a huge change in the diagnosis and management of multiple sclerosis, the biggest cause of nontraumatic neurological disability in young people in the United States. Though nothing currently cures or stops the disease, we have numerous therapies available that limit the damage done to the brain and spinal cord. These medications have changed the landscape of care in MS. The earlier the diagnosis is made, the sooner patients are able to get on medication. The sooner they are treated, the less damage is done by the disease.

Besides treatments that slow the disease, certain therapies help MS patients. Those with brain and spinal cord disease from MS can experience cognitive problems, chronic pain, bladder dysfunction, and mobility problems. The bladder dysfunction may not be able to be fixed, but there are techniques and medications that can dramatically improve the quality of life and decrease the restrictions placed on people when they suffer such bladder problems.

The cognitive deficits are problematic and difficult to change, but they can be prevented from worsening. Research into impaired cognition in MS and other neurodegenerative disorders is huge. Medications in the pipeline development stages and lifestyle changes including diet and exercise are being evaluated to help patients manage cognition and eventually slow the course of cognitive decline.

Chronic pain is an area of unmet need in nearly all fields of medicine. Pain is a difficult problem for a physician. Pain is useful; without it, we wouldn't survive very long. We wouldn't know when a bone was broken or when we had something like appendicitis or when our cornea was scratched. These can lead to infection and death if not caught.

But it can be tough to find the cause of chronic pain. The nerves are saying there's something wrong, but there actually isn't. This is useless pain, and it can be debilitating. It can cause loss of wages, unemployment, and disability. In health care, chronic pain is a huge area of unmet need, but it is also an area ripe for abuse in terms of prescription drugs and Social Security disability payments.

Since there are no objective tests to demonstrate what's causing chronic pain, physicians often have to take a patient's word for it. The physiology of chronic pain is difficult to understand. There are different philosophies as to its potential sources. One has to do with the biochemistry of neuro-peptides that are released chronically from cells for unknown reasons and then nerves send a signal to the brain, which interprets the signal as a pain source. The other thought has to do with a pain pathway in the brain that can't shut off; it continues in a chronic pain loop that the brain cannot stop. The brain continues to interpret pain when there is no reason for it. How and why these things occur is not understood completely. This is an area of medicine that requires research in terms of treatment and understanding.

These cases show that though something is not necessarily curable, there are measures physicians can take to help patients. In neurology as in life, we learn to manage our problems and search for a cure. We hope for answers and work to find them. We use the resources and evidence we have to distinguish between possibilities. We investigate options and build a case for the best explanation for the way things are. As in life, there is no easy answer; we must weigh the evidence to make the diagnosis. As self-conscious creatures, we can gain understanding of this world and use our knowledge and experience to determine if something makes the most sense.

Medical Apologetics

The remainder of this book will be dedicated to building a case for the existence of the God of the Bible and how He came to this earth in a human body to live, die, and rise for His creation. Just like making a difficult diagnosis in neurology where there are many possibilities and mimickers, the evidence tends to point to the most likely explanation. This is what I refer to as medical apologetics.

As I have pointed out previously, there is no single test to make a neurologic diagnosis, nor is there a test we can rely on 100 percent to include or exclude any diagnosis. The findings always have to fit into the context of the entire case.

The conclusion of each chapter will include a diagnosis, a physician's conclusion, an atheist's misdiagnosis, and an observational cohort analysis of each chapter. We will be comparing the two main worldviews of atheism and theism. It is important to review the basics of these briefly. Atheism will refer to the belief that there is no God and that all that exists came into being through evolutionary and naturalistic processes. Theism believes there is a God who created and sustains all existence; this is the view of Christians, Muslims, and Jews.

A third general worldview is polytheism. The polytheistic stance is more difficult and is generally any belief system in which there are multiple gods (Hinduism, Mormonism) or that everything is god, which is more accurately termed pantheism (new-age and cosmic humanism).

Since this book focuses mostly on whether the universe is more likely to have been designed and created rather than have come about by chance, atheism and theism will be the main, overarching views we will use to make up the diagnoses based on the evidence in each chapter. Based on the evidence for the views, we will make a case for the most likely explanation. Which view has the best overall and consistent explanations for the questions of the chapters? This is the thought process of a physician working up a new patient.

CHAPTER 4

Building the Case for a Diagnosis

When the apostles preached, they could assume even in their Pagan hearers a real consciousness of deserving the Divine anger. The Pagan mysteries existed to allay this consciousness, and the Epicurean philosophy claimed to deliver men from the fear of eternal punishment.

It was against this background that the Gospel appeared as good news. It brought good news of possible healing to men who knew that they were mortally ill. But all this has changed. Christianity now has to preach the diagnosis— in itself very bad news—before it can win a hearing for the cure. (Lewis C., The Problem of Pain, 1944, p. 48).

Case Report

A twenty-four-year-old, healthy female developed pain in one eye and over the next few hours began developing worsening vision in that eye; she saw a central dark gray spot. This continued through the day. The next morning, it was worse, so she saw her physician. The physician referred her to an ophthalmologist, who noticed she had some swelling in the back of the eye and astutely ordered a brain MRI thinking of an inflammatory CNS (central nervous system) disorder in a woman her age.

The brain MRI showed three white spots near the area of the brain called the corpus callosum. None of the spots showed enhancement with the intravenous contrast that she received. She was referred to a neurologist, who further evaluated her and diagnosed her with clinically isolated syndrome (a form of pre-MS).

Using Diagnostic Criteria to Make the Case for God

Do you ever wonder what it typically takes to convince a person of something? Why do some people easily accept certain things while other people are so resistant to them? Russian physicist Alexander Vilenkin stated, "It is said that an argument is what convinces reasonable men and a proof is what it takes to convince even an unreasonable man." (Vilenkin, 2006, p. 176). Other than in mathematics, it is difficult to actually prove anything. There seems to be an argument available against just about anything we say in this postmodern world. For example, if I say, "Lying is wrong," this seems like an easily accepted sentence. However, someone could say, "Who says lying is wrong? There's no such thing as truth anyway. If a person lies to save someone else, isn't lying right?"

There are many good ways to go about this problem and many good arguments to be made in these scenarios. We might first start with an argument demonstrating that truth exists and truth is objective. We might then discuss the moral-law argument and how that demonstrates that morals are not subjective for each person but are based on a standard. We might then use the argument for the authenticity of the Bible and how Jesus raised the bar for moral standards. We must be careful, however, to be winsome and gentle. We are instructed in 1 Peter 3:15 to explain with gentleness and respect. Our goal is not to win arguments but to help win souls for heaven. It's also our goal to refute bad philosophy and guide the argument to truth.

Just as neurologists collect all the information and data they can to build a case for the most likely cause of a patient's problems, we can examine the evidence and build a case for the best explanation of reality. Why are things the way they are? What is the origin of everything? What is the best coherent explanation consistent with reality?

Localization, Diagnostic Criteria, and Medical Epidemiology

In the prior chapter, I introduced the method of neurological localization during physical examination; in this chapter, I will review some techniques we can use to make observations and evaluate the evidence. We will apply that after we review the evidence throughout this book.

Let us look at a particular medical diagnostic set of criteria we use for diagnosing multiple sclerosis. Later in the chapter, we will review some medical epidemiological tools for evaluating observations including cohort studies and causal inference. Toward the end of each chapter, we will come back to these techniques and apply them to the evidence we have discovered along the way to determine what the best explanations for the observations are. We will apply these three approaches to help systematize and weigh the evidence for the existence of God as the best explanation and the diagnosis—the cause of existence. At the end, we will determine whether the associations are causally related.

MS Criteria and the Existence of God

Let's begin with applying the clinical diagnostic criteria of a definite diagnosis of relapsing MS to the arguments for or against a creator of the universe. We could just as easily use other criteria such as those to diagnosis Parkinson's disease or ALS. I chose the MS diagnostic criteria because it offers different levels of certainty based on the evidence. It also included methods to help exclude diagnoses that may cause similar symptoms.

As discussed earlier, MS is an inflammatory and progressively degenerative disease of the brain and spinal cord. The inflammation causes loss of myelin (the insulating layer around many nerves) and can cause severe injury and death to brain cells. It most commonly begins causing symptoms in young people in their forties. In terms of diagnosis, the current and most widely accepted diagnostic criteria is called the 2010 McDonald Criteria for MS (Polman, 2011). According to the criteria, a person would be diagnosed with possible, probable, definite, or no MS.

As is the case with most other neurological disorders, there is no single test that will give us the answer; if only it were as simple as that. We must rely on several clinical factors. The diagnosis is fundamentally based on two clinical/historical events typical of MS and two objective clinical findings on the neurological exam that correspond to the historical events. This is to exclude other possible explanations or mimickers of MS.

In addition, brain and cervical MRI can be (and usually are) performed to help make the confirmation. If there is still suspicion and further evaluation is required, the cerebrospinal fluid (CSF) can be tapped to search for evidence of MS and inflammation in the brain and spinal cord. Another test called visual evoked potentials is performed to evaluate the functioning of the optic nerves to determine if there is loss of myelin in those regions. This can be summarized in this way:

Definite diagnosis: dissemination in space and time

Evidence of 2 clinical/historical events (optic neuritis, transverse myelitis, brain stem syndrome)
Evidence of 2 objective neurological exam findings that corresponds to the history
+/- brain or cervical MRI evidence
One other possible way to make this diagnosis is if there are active and old lesions on one single brain MRI at the same time.

Probable diagnosis: dissemination in space or time

Evidence of 1–2 clinical/historical events
Evidence of 1–2 corresponding objective exam findings
Evidence of lesions on the brain or spinal cord consistent with CNS demyelination

Possible diagnosis:

1 clinical/historical event
or 1 objective exam finding
or brain/spinal cord MRI with lesions suspicious for CNS demyelination
CSF evidence of inflammation or MS
visual evoked potential evidence of optic nerve demyelination

No MS
no objective findings with a normal brain/cervical MRI and normal CSF
better explained by something else

These diagnostic criteria are extremely beneficial for neurologists to help include or exclude difficult cases. In medicine, there are medical errors and misdiagnoses. In apologetics, there are difficulties in answering tough historical and philosophical questions. No single piece of evidence will usually suffice, but based on all the evidence, we can make a very good case one way or another.

The young woman at the beginning of this chapter had several lesions on her brain MRI and inflammation in the nerve at the back of the eye, but that still does not meet the criteria of definite MS. It will take more information over time to add to that case, but we can make very good conclusions and consequently base treatment decisions on the information.

Validity of Tests

To determine what the validity of a test or study in medicine actually is, we refer to measures in statistics called sensitivity and specificity. These statistics refer to the ability of a certain test to detect and rule in the correct diagnosis accurately or the strength to be able to rule out other diagnoses accurately.

For example, the specificity of the 2010 revised McDonald criteria to accurately exclude a patient who truly does not have MS is 93 percent. That means that based on just meeting these criteria, a person without MS will have a 93 percent chance of the test correctly demonstrating this.

This also means there will be few false negatives. The sensitivity is about 74 percent, which means that it is good at correctly diagnosing the disorder in someone with MS. Another example of sensitivity would be if there were 100 people who had a known diagnosis of MS, then the 2010 revised McDonald criteria would correctly diagnose 74 of them. And if 100 people without MS were tested with this criteria, 93 of them would be correctly found to not have MS. It is important to remember that there are no tests in medicine that have 100 percent specificity or sensitivity. The gold standard for any condition has high specificity and sensitivity alike.

It is also important to note it's not possible to prove the existence or nonexistence of God. We make the most plausible conclusions based on the data. The plausibility of the interpretation of the data is what should drive the conclusion; applying diagnostic principles with strong diagnostic accuracy to the data can add weight to the argument.

Value of Tests

Even more important than the validity of a test is its ability to predict the correct outcome. This is termed either the positive predictive value (PPV) or the negative predictive value (NPV). A test with a strong PPV will appropriately be positive and have fewer false positives. A test with a strong NPV will correctly determine that if a person tests negative for a disorder, he or she does not have it. Here's an example of PPV. If 1,000 people are tested for a disorder and 180 of them test positive but only 80 actually have the disease, PPV is 44 percent (the true positives divided by the true positives plus the false positives).

The PPV of the 2010 McDonald criteria has been reported to be approximately 94 percent and its NPV is roughly 70 percent (Belova, 2014). This means that if a person actually has MS, the 2010 McDonald criteria will have a 94 percent chance of being positive for MS. If a person does not have MS, the diagnostic criteria will have a 70 percent chance of correctly diagnosing no MS.

Is there a gold standard for testing different belief systems and worldviews? Is there a way to measure one person's beliefs against another's? This may not be a simple thing to do, and it may not be perfect, but the gold standard is to hold each worldview against the backdrop of reality. Compare each worldview and the way the world is and see which one comes up best and which ones come up short.

For example, which belief system best explains where we came from, why we are here, why the things are the way they are, what do we do to fix it, and what happens after we die? But there is more to it than just answering those questions; each of the answers needs to be internally consistent with the other answers. If our existence is best explained by random collocation of atoms having come to together by unguided forces, that indicates things are the way they are because of natural selection and self-interest and self-survival. This short life is all there is, and the earth along with the universe will one day be a cold, lifeless graveyard of dead planets and used-up stars. If that is the case, there is no ultimate purpose.

If you believe that, why live as if there were meaning and purpose in your choices? That is not consistent. This method of testing worldviews is grounded mostly in philosophy and is probably the best model to evaluate them well.

Can We Treat Worldviews As We Do Diseases?

Using the gold-standard method of diagnostics in medicine, is it possible to utilize this strategy to diagnose the most likely worldview? By applying the principles of diagnostics and epidemiology to apologetics, can we create an argument for the most likely worldview? Let's go back to the 2010 revised McDonald criteria for MS diagnosis. We can weigh the evidence and make a differential diagnosis. Is it more likely that atheism or theism is the best explanation?

The MS Criteria Is Good for Evaluating God

Positive predictive value is a beneficial way of determining the strength of a test; it is affected by two factors: the prevalence of a disease in a population and the specificity of the test. If the prevalence of disease is high, the PPV will be high. If the specificity is high, the PPV will be high. In this book, we will be testing the given observational evidence with a low prevalence of disease so the specificity of the test will be more important. Since the specificity of the McDonald criteria is very high at 93 percent and the PPV is high at 94 percent, this is a great tool to evaluate the strength of the evidence of a creator.

Observations and Evidence

Each of the chapters will review (not exhaustively) the observations we make about the universe and existence and some of the arguments behind the explanations of these observations. In medicine, we make observations in multiple ways such as with physical examinations, the patients' medical histories, and their symptoms. We evaluate the observations by running tests to narrow the potential field of possibilities and come up with the best explanation.

Testing the Observations (Cohort Studies)

At the conclusion of each chapter, there will be an observational study to determine whether the evidence is related to a potential cause or not. The cohort study is a common model for determining an association between an exposure such as smoking and its relation to an outcome in a population such as lung cancer. Basically, a cohort study will investigate a trait or exposure over time and observe the outcomes.

The most famous cohort study is the Framingham study that began in Framingham, Massachusetts in 1948. This study has generated over 1,000 medical publications based on cardiovascular risk factors and lifestyle effects on morbidity. Cohort studies are very helpful in revealing if certain factors are associated with the observations we see. To determine if there is a relationship between an exposure and a disorder in medical epidemiology, we must determine whether the factor and the development of something have an association and whether that association is causally related. Some associations may appear that they are real but are actually considered spurious or confounded. For example, many people who develop MS do not eat much fish; many people who do not eat fish tend to live in landlocked areas where more red meat is consumed. The consumption of less fish is not directly related to the development of MS, but it may be associated indirectly.

We make inferences and collect evidence based on the observations. We then test the evidence to see if there is an association between the observations and the disorder. If there is an association, we then must ask whether it is real or spurious. If we determine it is real, we must determine if the association is causally related. To test the evidence, we design studies. Cohort studies are performed to determine if there is evidence of a relationship between an observation and an exposure. A cohort study compares a population of people exposed to a certain factor (smoking for example) and observes which people develop the disease (lung cancer). There are four potential outcome groups.

1. exposed and developed the disease (outcome 1)
2. exposed and did not develop the disease (outcome 2)
3. not exposed and developed the disease (outcome 1)
4. not exposed and did not develop the disease (outcome 2)

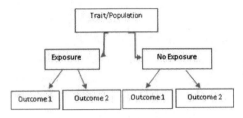

Figure 2: Generic cohort design

A cohort study will test the evidence of the observation and determine if there is an association between the observation and the exposure. If there is a positive association, we would expect the ratio of the people who were exposed and developed the disease to be greater than the people who were not exposed and developed the disease.

Study Design

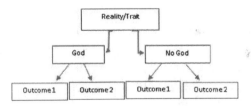

Figure 3. Outcome based on the exposure of reality to God versus no God

The creation of the particular design of a study is the key for evaluating the evidence. Poorly designed studies do not make compelling arguments. Studies in medicine with the least weight are considered anecdotal case studies and series. These add some new experiences but do not necessarily change the way medicine is implemented.

Physicians must be very careful in taking too much away from case studies because we cannot extrapolate much evidence from just one case to treat patients, but they are helpful in that they add some new insights and can lead to more well-designed and generalized controlled studies.

In this book, we will be focusing on observations made through science and nature and examining them. The design of the study will be retrospective (historical) and a modified cohort. Because we are not studying a population, we will be using a modified cohort to determine a potential relationship. The exposure will be God and the unexposed will be No God. These could easily be switched, but it makes more sense to keep it that way.

To determine if there is an association between what we see and exposure, we will determine which evidence is more likely to fit in the exposed and diseased category versus the not exposed and diseased category. To make an association, the proportion of exposed and diseased must be greater than the unexposed and diseased.

Causal Inference

If an association is made, we can determine whether the association is causally related.

1. Temporal relation: Was the cause prior to the effect?
2. Strength: The higher the probability, the more likely it is causal
3. Replication of findings: We would expect to see the same thing in other groups and populations.
4. Alternative explanations: Are there multiple plausible explanations?
5. Cessation of exposure: If the removal of the cause decreases the effect, it is causal.

Sufficient and Necessary Causes

If a causal relationship is established, there are different strengths of this relationship. A cause may be sufficient and/or necessary or neither. There are four possible pathways of causal relationships.

1. necessary and sufficient
2. necessary but not sufficient

3. not necessary but sufficient
4. neither necessary nor sufficient

Necessary refers to a factor that has to be present for a disease to occur. Without the factor, the disease does not occur. Sufficient means that if the factor is present, it always occurs, but this is not common with diseases. Even the most infectious viruses do not always cause disease in all people exposed (for instance, some people are immune to HIV). Some causes are necessary but not sufficient. Certain genes are likely to cause a disease such as multiple sclerosis, but by themselves, they do not cause the disease. The genes may be necessary but are not sufficient; they need more factors including environmental exposures to viruses or low levels of vitamin D.

Some causes are sufficient but not necessary. This is the case when there are many causes for the same disease. For example, skin cancer can be hereditary or caused by sun overexposure, chemical exposure, etc. Each exposure is sufficient to cause the disease but not necessary. Many causes are neither necessary nor sufficient, and this is probably the case in most chronic diseases such as Alzheimer's disease, in which different genetic and environmental factors all play roles and none is by itself necessary or sufficient.

Over the next several chapters, we will review the observations and the evidence and possible explanations for the things we see and experience. After reviewing this information, we will evaluate the evidence in the diagnostic criteria for MS, determine if there is an association between potential causes and the observations, and determine if the association is causally related.

PART II

THE EVIDENCE

CHAPTER 5

Who Created God?

By faith we understand that the universe was created by the word of God, so that what is seen has been made from things that are not visible.

—Hebrews 11:3

Bertrand Russell said,

> I may say that when I was a young man and was debating these questions very seriously in my mind, I for a long time accepted the argument of the First Cause, until one day, at the age of eighteen, I read John Stuart Mill's Autobiography, and I there found this sentence: "My father taught me that the question 'Who made me?' cannot be answered, since it immediately suggests the further question 'Who made god?'" That very simple sentence showed me, as I still think, the fallacy in the argument of the First Cause. If everything must have a cause, then God must have a cause. (Russell, 1927).

This chapter will deal with several questions that deal with origins and the beginning of things. Why we are here and where did anything come from are fundamental questions that every seeker desires to know. Questions about the seemingly impossibility of the origin of life by chance and the question of why things seem to be so bad will be addressed in later chapters.

In medicine, we are trained to gather data from patients and their families in regard to the time and course of events leading to their problems as well as other history that may play a role. For example, when people who are having seizures go to neurologists, the doctors will always go into detail in their search for any clues or reasons for the seizures. They will ask about their birth histories and any complications surrounding that. They will find out if they met all their developmental milestones appropriately or if there were challenges. They will search for other possible signs of seizures as an infant related to high fevers. They will gather prior history about other family members with question of seizures or other disorders.

None of these things alone will give us the answer sufficiently, but they can build a case for or against a seizure in a patient. A history of brain infection or head traumas will add weight. In apologetics, gathering information and history helps build a case for the appropriate and best explanation as well.

Cosmology

Cosmology is a branch of astrophysics that studies the universe on a large scale. We begin with things that exist and work our way back to why they exist in the first place. There are philosophical and scientific data that drive the cosmological arguments of the origin of time, matter, and life. This area of apologetics deals best with trying to find explanations for important questions such as what caused the universe to begin and where information comes from. The answers to these questions start building the case for the best worldview.

Cosmological Arguments

I will review there three fundamental cosmological arguments for the existence of God, but this is not exhaustive. For more information regarding these and others, there are many great resources including *Reasonable Faith* by William Lane Craig (Craig, Reasonable Faith: Christian Truth and

Apologetics 3rd Edition, 2008) and *The Handbook of Christian Apologetics* by Peter Kreeft and Ronald K. Tacelli (Kreeft, 1994).

These are not new arguments, but with the help of recent apologetics, they have gained steam and some fresh air. Craig has had a huge impact on the usefulness of several of these arguments, especially the Kalam cosmological argument for which he has literally written the book (Craig, The Kalam Cosmological Argument, 1979). Simply put, kalam is an Arabic term that refers to the defense of theology.

It is important to state why these arguments are so critical. Atheists believe the universe is all there is. According to atheism, nothing created the universe. It has always existed or created itself out of nothing. Quentin Smith states in *The Cambridge Companion to Atheism*, "I argue that the cause of the universe's beginning is not God but the universe itself. More precisely, I argue that the universe's beginning to exist is *self-caused*" (Martin, 2007, p. 184). Or atheists will say that it is just impossible for the universe to have an explanation. According to theism, a being beyond time and space must have created everything that exists. If atheism is true, the universe did not have a creator but has always existed or came into being out of nothing. This is crucial; the answer to this question of the origin of matter and life is fundamental to the way we will answer all other questions regarding the nature of human beings as well.

If human beings are nothing but chance and atoms, it doesn't matter whether we exist. There is no ultimate purpose of our existence or the existence of anything. But if according to the Christian theist, we are made in the image of God, the *imago Dei*, we are highly valued beings with ultimate value and meaning.

Does Nothing Exist?

What is nothing? It can't even be imagined. Yet naturalists claim that the universe came into existence from nothing by nothing. As William Lane Craig says, "That is worse than magic!" Scientists know that nothing comes from nothing. The ancient Greeks realized that fact with the statement that became in Latin *Ex nihilo nihil fit*—out of nothing, nothing comes. It is common sense. The highly speculative "scientific" claims that the universe created itself out of nothing is absurd.

When the term *nothing* is used, be careful that the person using it is actually referring to nothing. The definition of nothing is the absence of anything. It clearly does not and cannot exist. It is not possible to even say that nothing exists because the existence of anything is something. When physicists say nothing created the universe, they are referring to something such as energy and vacuum fluctuations, but that is not nothing. Where did those things come from?

Thomas Aquinas (1225–1274) is considered an eminent church father; he is credited with several critical ideas that fuse faith and reason. He became a Dominican and studied theology and philosophy; he was determined to find "proofs" for the existence of God. We will discuss his ideas and move into other cosmological arguments. His first and basic argument can be summarized as

1. The universe exists.
2. The existence of the universe has a cause.
   The cause is God. (Samuel, 2010)

The first premise is based on our perception that reality exists. We see, taste, feel, hear, and smell the world around us and experience it. We see the trees and the colors of the flowers. We know things exist. We know gravity exists; it is easy to test for it. The denial of the existence of the universe is absurd. There are, however, many philosophers who have argued for the denial of the universe. Certain world religions such as some Eastern forms including Buddhism deny the existence of the material world and call much of matter an illusion. Most honest investigators will agree that the first premise is true.

The second premise—the existence of the universe has a cause—is more complex. This has been hotly debated over time. Before the discovery of several important scientific breakthroughs, it was easier to state that the universe was eternal or it has just existed. However, that is no longer the case. Since Einstein's theory of general relativity and the discovery of the Hubble constant and cosmic microwave background radiation, we know the universe has not always existed and that it along with time has a beginning. Since the universe has a beginning, it has a cause.

One way Aquinas attempted to demonstrate this is through the argument of causality—if something exists, it must have a cause. He used the argument of motion to illustrate this. If something is moving, it must have had something start it in motion and something that continues its motion. For example, instead of just thinking of a ball hitting another ball to make it move, Aquinas suggests thinking about a set of gears the first of which makes the others move and sustains their movement.

Bertrand Russell's argument against this claim is that if everything has a cause, God also has a cause. Russell stated that was one question he could not get past; it led him into his unbelief in God. This argument will be addressed in later portions of the cosmological arguments and is easily refuted based on further understanding of the creator's nature.

The third premise has to do with God as the creator of the universe. At first glance, this argument seems to jump right to a crazy conclusion that God has to be the explanation. Right away, this seems like a leap; it raises eyebrows and begs the question, "Why does the cause have to be God?" Can't there be another possible cause for the beginning of time and matter? Aquinas understood God to be the perfect and infinite being that created everything. God is the uncreated creator. No one created God. If there were something greater than God that created God, that would be God, and on and on. There must be a first uncaused cause.

The Kalam Cosmological Argument

In their *Cambridge Companion for Atheism*, atheist Quentin Smith stated the importance of Dr. William Lane Craig and his defense of this argument.

A count of the articles in philosophy journals shows that more articles have been published about Craig's defense of the Kalam cosmological argument than have been published about any other philosopher's contemporary formulation of an argument for God's existence ... Theists and atheists alike cannot leave Craig's Kalam argument alone. (Martin, 2007)

This compelling and powerful argument originated in the twelfth century AD and was formulated by Muhammad Al-Ghazali, a Muslim philosopher (Craig, On Guard; Defending your faith with reason and precision, 2010). The argument is summarized this way.

1. Whatever begins to exist has a cause.
2. The universe began to exist.
3. The universe has a cause.

The first premise seems obvious. An important point is that it does not state, "Everything that exists has a cause." Some atheists misuse this argument to make their point that even God must have a cause. Like Bertrand Russell, they erroneously come to the conclusion that Christians are then forced to come up with an explanation for God. The first premise is that anything that has a beginning must have a cause. Again, this is obvious. This is the way the world works as we know it; we do not see objects or life coming into existence from nowhere. As pointed out earlier, this is the understanding even from ancient Greek philosophy.

Time Is Not Infinite

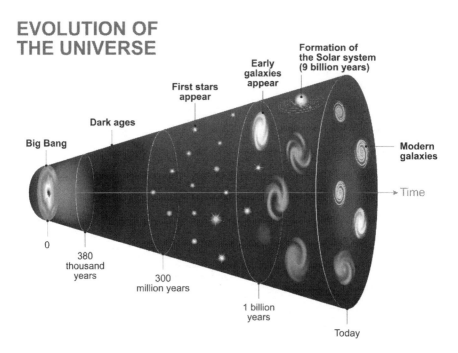

EVOLUTION OF THE UNIVERSE

Based on our current understanding of the origin of the universe, time also had a beginning. Time seems to be "stitched" into matter and space. Time began with the big bang. Even before modern science has reinforced this idea, Al-Ghazali understood this as well as the fact that time must have had a beginning. For example, if time were infinite, time would never have reached the present day. Just as it is impossible to count to infinity, it is also impossible to count down from infinity. Since time is not infinite, it must have had a beginning. Something beyond or outside of time must exist to begin it.

The Universe Is Matter

Since the universe is made up of space and matter, it began to exist. We know from big bang cosmology that the universe began at some point. This raises the question, "What caused the universe to exist?" Physicist Stephen Hawking stated, "Because there is a law like gravity, the universe can and will create itself from nothing" (Hawking, 2010). It is somewhat shocking to hear brilliant scientists and professors state these sorts of things. We think, *Clearly, Stephen Hawking must know something I don't. He's obviously a very brilliant scientist. He's definitely able to comprehend things I probably could never understand.* I ask myself, *Is there some way Stephen Hawking thinks about the initial universe I just can't grasp?* This is intimidating when such brilliant people come up with claims such as these and we feel we have to take them at their word. Well, when I read *The Grand Design* by Hawking and his coauthor, Leonard Mlodinow, I found it very interesting in terms of the basic science and physics review, but I rolled my eyes at some of their conclusions. I do not understand the statement that anything "can and will create itself." We all know from common sense that this does not and will not happen.

The atheist will argue, "Hawking is talking about quantum physics, and quantum physics does not act like classical physics." That may be the case, but just because so-called quantum physics is unpredictable and improbable, that gives us no explanation of how something could create itself. There is nothing that can create itself. That would mean it must have been present prior to itself to create itself. It is amazing that anyone would even make this argument. Hawking also states that because of a law like gravity, the universe will create itself. Where did gravity come from?

Atheists Believe in Miracles

Which is harder to believe—that the universe was created out of nothing by nothing or that the universe was created out of nothing by something? Those who say something as complex and amazing as the universe came from nothing by chance are basically saying they believe in magic. As William Lane Craig states, "To claim that something can come into being from nothing is worse than magic. When a magician pulls a rabbit out of a hat, at least you've got the magician, not to mention the hat!" (Craig, Reasonable Faith, 2014).

Why do atheists continue to attempt to come up with reasons that the universe is not created? Why are they trying so hard to come up with reasons that the universe either created itself or has always existed? Why not admit that the best explanation is a timeless, spaceless, immaterial, powerful, personal, sustaining creator? What are the implications of accepting this? This means that there is accountability. This means that we must make big changes to the way we live our lives. We are no longer able to live just by our desires and instincts; we must realize our actions matter and we will need to change our lives based on that fact.

In Luke 14, Jesus said, "If anyone comes to me and does not hate his own father and mother, wife and children—yes, and even his own life—he cannot be My disciple. Whoever does not bear his own cross and come after Me cannot be My disciple." Jesus was not telling us to hate our family members; that would clearly be inconsistent with His teaching. He was telling us that compared to everything in life—all our relationships, possessions, the whole world—is nothing compared to the surpassing love and relationship of our Lord and God. Using hyperbole, He demonstrated the great love we must be aware of when we come into relationship with the Father. Compared to the love of the Father, our relationships in this life are basically meaningless. He was saying we must not be too attached to any person or thing in this life; we must be willing to give it all up for our Lord.

In Ecclesiastes 3:11, the author stated that God had "placed eternity in their hearts." We have the understanding that there is something more than this world. Despite Carl Sagan's statement that the cosmos is all that is, was, or will be, we know otherwise. Our hearts tell us that the cosmos is not all there is.

Sufficient Reason

The final argument from cosmology has been refined over the ages and has to do with sufficient reason. This was best explained by Gottfried Wilhelm Leibniz (1646–1716), a German mathematician and philosopher. His argument is summarized as follows.

1. Anything that exists has an explanation of its existence either in a necessity of its own nature to exist or in an external cause outside itself.
2. If the universe has an explanation of its existence, that explanation is God.
3. The universe exists.

Based on these premises, what follows is the conclusion that since the universe exists and whatever exists has an explanation of its existence, the explanation of the universe is God. This argument is very compelling, but several questions come to mind. Why does the explanation of the universe have to be God? Couldn't there be something else to explain it? Can't the universe exist necessarily?

I think that it is helpful to explain the first premise more. Leibniz did not say that everything that exists has an explanation for its existence except God. He states that everything that exists has an explanation for why it exists—either because it was caused by something else or because its very nature was to exist. So what is meant by existing by its own nature? Something that exists necessarily means it is impossible for it not to exist. This gives a very powerful concept for the definition of God. If anything created God, that would have been God. No one can come up with a concept greater than the concept of God. If they could, that would be God. God cannot cease to exist. God is the greatest comprehensible being.

Couldn't the Universe Exist Necessarily?

Most atheists do not think the universe necessarily exists. We know the universe had a beginning, so it does not exist necessarily. As stated before, something that necessarily exists cannot fail to exist. But most atheists agree that it is possible this universe could not have come into existence. Craig gives the example that we can all think of other universes, and since we can think of other universes and that does nothing to change this one, this universe does not exist necessarily.

Why Does the Explanation Have to Be God?

If the universe exists and it has an explanation for its existence, the explanation is something timeless, spaceless, and immaterial. Only two things fit that description. One is God, and the other is an abstract object such as a number. But we know that numbers and other abstract objects don't cause anything to exist. When was the last time the number twelve made anything happen?

The Implications

This raises the idea that there cannot be an infinite number of things that exist that are contingent. There must be something that exists first that did not require a cause, or else this leads to an infinite regression of causes. Since we know things don't pop into existence out of nothing and everything must have a cause either necessarily or from an external cause, there must be a necessary being. This is the idea of the principle of sufficient reason.

Differential Diagnosis

Theism and atheism offer explanations for the origins of the universe. Worldviews that consider reality illusory such as some forms of polytheism and pantheism do not offer sufficient evidence for where anything comes from or why things exist. In fact, if this is all an illusion as some Eastern religions suggest, science is also an illusion and any discovery of the origin of time or reality is not real. This argument does not hold up. With cosmic humanism, everything is spirit and matter is only a manifestation of spirit. Ultimate reality is considered spiritual rather than physical unlike naturalism.

According to cosmic humanism, all truth is arrived at differently and our interpretation of reality differs. One cosmic humanist states,

> All that is can form itself into individual droplets of consciousness. Because you are part of all that is, you have literally always been, yet there was the instant when that individual energy current that is you was formed. Consider that the ocean is God. It has always been. Now reach in and grab a cup full of water. In that instant, the cup becomes individual, but it has always been, has it not? This is the case of your soul. (Zukav, 1989)

This does not explain why things exist. The reasonable options in the differential for the explanation of the origin of the universe include atheism and theism. Here is the weight of the diagnostic criteria so far.

Atheism (none of these is consistent with the others)	Theism (all of these are consistent with each other)
• Time and matter came into existence from nothing and by nothing.	• Time and matter came into existence from nothing by something.
• The universe just exists; the cosmos is all that ever was or ever will be.	• The universe was created by a necessary being.
• The universe has always existed.	• The universe had a beginning.

The diagnostic conclusion from cosmological arguments would place theism as more probable than atheism based on consistency and overall intelligibility. It is logical that it is more likely something comes into existence from nothing by something. It makes no sense to believe otherwise.

The Physician's Conclusion

Several historical symptoms can be explained and described by patients that fit with the diagnosis of MS. However, most symptoms people have are not specific to anything let alone MS. For example, if someone has numbness and tingling in the right hand as well as new headaches, the patient can put these symptoms into an online symptom checker or Google and get a potential response. The automated response may tell the person he or she has MS, but the more likely diagnosis may be carpal tunnel syndrome and tension headaches both of which are much more common separately and together than is MS.

However, if that person has symptoms of a black spot in the vision in one eye that came on over a couple of days and hurts when he or she moves the eye, and if that person included that fact in an online symptoms checker, the differential narrows dramatically and MS seems more likely. As a matter of fact, that sounds a lot like inflammation of the optic nerve. Now that may help, but we need to place that single piece of data in the whole context of the patient to know more about this.

If the patient is a twenty-two-year-old female who has been otherwise healthy, that would make inflammation of the optic nerve more likely than MS. But if the patient is a seventy-two-year-old man with rheumatism who smokes, this may fit better with something such as temporal arteritis or a diabetic retinopathy (I apologize for the medical jargon. Temporal arteritis refers to inflammation of an artery near the temple and diabetic retinopathy refers to blood vessel problems in the eye related to diabetes). An isolated piece of evidence does not help a whole lot except to start to build a case for an explanation.

In terms of the cosmological arguments, in the context of the cause of matter, space, and time, no physician would get away with telling a patient his or her symptoms just exist and came from nowhere by nothing. That is absurd and unacceptable. Based on diagnostic training just like in medicine, there must be an explanation, and the best explanation wins. There must be a cause of the universe, and it is a much better explanation to say something caused the universe than to say nothing caused the universe. To say that nothing caused the universe out of nothing is to say that you really don't know and you really don't care.

The Atheist's Misdiagnosis

The atheist misses the diagnosis quite dramatically on this one. As I have pointed out earlier, atheists will approach the premises to these arguments from the preconceived standpoint that God does not exist though the most probable conclusion to these arguments is that there is something that caused matter and time to exist.

Based on their presuppositions, atheists must believe the universe caused itself to exist or came into being out of nothing by nothing. These are both less probable than the idea there is a timeless, spaceless, necessary being that created the universe. Physicians weigh the evidence, and the most likely results will help formulate the differential diagnosis. A timeless, spaceless, necessary being is at the top of the differential. Patients are not satisfied when I tell them "It just happened" when I give them the diagnosis; they want an explanation. Most patients do not accept the claim that they developed a disease from nothing and by nothing. We all know things don't work that way.

Cohort Study

We know that nothing does not explain anything. Using the true definition of nothing, the absence of anything, it is obvious that something does not come to exist without something else. The existence of anything has to be explained either in a necessity of its nature to exist or in an external cause outside itself.

Since we know the universe exists, with cohort 1, it is easy to see that a timeless and spaceless creator can cause everything to exist *ex nihilo*. But with cohort 2, only outcome 2 is possible. If outcome 1 is possible with cohort 1 but not with cohort 2, we can make the association that cohort 1 is necessary for the existence of the universe. Since we know that nothing exists without something, God must exist. Without something to cause everything, there would be nothing. This isn't rocket science.

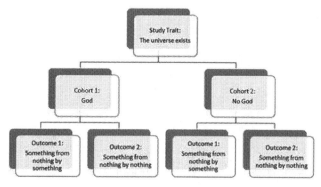

Figure 4: Cohort study evaluating observations
based on the existence of the universe

It is quite clear that many people do not want to accept that a personal creator exists and would rather believe that which is philosophically and scientifically impossible. Without something that is beyond space and time, nothing would exist. Something personal rather than abstract has to choose to make something exist from nothing. Without God, nothing exists, and that is not what we observe.

CHAPTER 6

Where Do Morals Come From?

Christianity spoke again and said: "I have always maintained that men were naturally backsliders; that human virtue tended of its own nature to rust or to rot; I have always said that human beings as such go wrong, especially happy human beings, especially proud and prosperous human beings. This eternal revolution, this suspicion sustained through centuries, you (being a vague modern) call the doctrine of progress. If you were a philosopher you would call it, as I do, the doctrine of original sin. You may call it cosmic advance as much as you like; I call it what it is—the Fall." (Chesterton, Orthodoxy, 1908)

Before diving in too deep into this topic, let us review and define some terms. We may all speak the same language, but we tend to use different dictionaries. Morals are the objective values and duties humans inherently apply to other humans and actions. Values refer to the worth of a person or action as either good or bad. Duties refer to the obligation to act in a certain way either right or wrong (Craig, 2010).

Objective refers to a standard we can all measure from. How could anyone say Mother Teresa acted any better than Adolf Hitler did? Without an objective standard, it would be a person's opinion. Why are murder, rape, and adultery considered wrong? Why are beauty, love, and patience considered right? Are these just matters of personal preference? Are they constructed from sociobiological conditioning? Are we just taught these things through culture, or do we all somehow know these intrinsic truths?

Subjective refers to someone's personal preference. For example, I love chocolate. It's objectively true I love chocolate, but it is not objectively true that chocolate is better than vanilla (though I cannot understand how anyone couldn't think so). It is my personal preference. On a more serious note, someone may say that torturing children for fun is not wrong. What? Well, based on naturalism, it really wouldn't be wrong. This is inconsistent, as we will see.

House Hunter Morality

For whatever reason, my wife and I enjoy watching *House Hunters* on cable. Real exciting, I know, but we like the show. The first five minutes introduces a couple; viewers find out what each of them desires in a home. We learn about their budget and location, and then we watch as they explore three homes that meet each of their desires differently. Near the end of the show but before the couple has chosen which house they plan to purchase, we get to bet on which one we think they will choose. Not surprisingly, when my four-year-old daughter joins this game, she usually wins.

This process of choosing what we want based on personal preference rather than what is true or useful seems to permeate our culture and our sense of how we see the world. Which morality am I going to choose today? 1, 2, or 3? Is this morality useful for me or not? Rather, we should be looking not at morals as a way to suit our conscience; our sense of right and wrong should fit the way things are. A correct sense of morality does not force undue judgment on anyone. It is not an argument about my morals or your morals; it is an argument about *the* morals. The correct morals are the objective standard by which we measure right and wrong.

Man in Black

At our neuroscience clinic, every Thursday is Johnny Cash Day. This is mostly just for fun (and it makes wardrobe selections easy one day a week). It makes for a good topic of discussion briefly with patients and their families as well. But it is also a reminder that things aren't the way we think they should be. There is something in each of us that knows when some things are right or wrong. In his song "Man in Black," Johnny Cash explained why he wore black.

> I wear the black for the poor and beaten down, livin' in the hopeless, hungry side of town.
> I wear it for the prisoner who is long paid for his crime, but is there because he's a victim of the times.
> I wear the black for those who've never read or listened to the words that Jesus said about the road to happiness through love and charity.
> Why, you'd think He's talking straight to you and me.

We know certain things are not right, but how do we know that? Where does that sense come from? Atheism doesn't explain that. To the naturalist, our biochemistry sends, receives, and coordinates signals that result in behaviors. This is described by scientific determinism and means that the behaviors and actions of people are the result of biochemistry. When there are unbeneficial behaviors, there must have been some wrong signals sent or interpreted. The physical is all there is. There is no free will. According to naturalism, we really don't even have choices; the perception of our decisions is just biochemistry.

Argument from Morality

Without objective value and duty, there is no way to gauge anything; everything would just be a subjective preference. If there is no objective standard for right and wrong or good and bad, it is all just subjective. So why should I listen to you or believe you? The argument from morality can be illustrated in this way.

1. If God does not exist, objective moral values and duties do not exist.
2. Objective moral values and duties do exist.
3. God exists.

Ravi Zacharias has formulated an explanation for those who ask, "How can a loving and all-powerful God allow such evil?" He wrote,

> In order for there to be evil, you are assuming there is good. If you are assuming there is good, then you are assuming there must be an objective moral law or standard on which to measure between evil and good. If there is an objective moral law or standard, then there must be a moral law giver. But that is who you're trying to disprove and not prove. If there is no moral law giver, then there is no moral law. If there is no moral law, then there is no good. If there is no good, then there is no evil. What is your question? (Zacharias, 2016).

No Good?

Richard Dawkins claimed, "The universe we observe has precisely the properties we should expect if there is, at bottom, no design, no purpose, no evil, no good, nothing but blind, pitiless indifference" (Dawkins, River Out of Eden: A Darwinian View of Life, 1995). This is an astonishing statement. Does anyone really believe that? Does Dawkins really believe that? Does this really give the best explanation for the way the world is? Does this give anyone a good explanation for why anything is the way that it is? Fyodor Dostoyevsky said, "If God does not exist, then everything is permissible."

Atheists know that some things are not permissible, and they clearly do not live as though everything were permissible. Peter Kreeft states,

> Most of us, whatever our religious faith, or lack of it, can recognize that in the life of someone like Francis of Assisi human nature is operating the right way, the way it ought

to operate. You need not be a theist to see *that* St. Francis's life was admirable, but you need to be a theist to see *why*. (Kreeft, 1994)

Where Do Morals Come From?

Most people don't buy the idea that morals came from lifeless matter and the random collocation of particles over time. That does nothing to explain why some things are right or wrong. Peter Kreeft gives an illustration.

> Many scientists examine secondary causes all their lives without acknowledging the First Cause, God. But, as we have seen, those secondary causes could not *be* without the First Cause, even though they can be *known* without knowing the First Cause. The same is true of objective moral good. (Kreeft, 1994)

Atheists are inconsistent in their views and actions. If no moral objectives exist, why do atheists act as moral activists? Why does Dawkins speak up for the oppressed? According to his explanations, it's not wrong for people to be oppressed, but he doesn't live that way nor do any of his fellow atheists.

Batman versus Superman

When I saw the trailer for the movie *Batman vs. Superman*, I thought, *What? How could anyone think there was another superhero who could beat superman? How could anyone think a mortal could beat Superman? Why did a producer and director even attempt a movie like that?* It made no sense to me. Superman is unbeatable. He is good and strong, and no other superhero can even get close to beating him let alone a mere man like Bruce Wayne.

I finally saw the movie and figured out why. Toward the end of the movie, Lex Luther says to Superman, "I figured out, way back, that if

God is all-powerful, He cannot be all good. And if He is all good, then He cannot be all-powerful. And neither can you be … black and blue. God versus man. Day versus night." The Lex Luther character uses the age-old argument that an all-loving and all-powerful God cannot exist if evil exists. This movie is another man vs. God battle. The battle of morals. The theological naïveté is clear. Let's look at this argument more closely.

All-Powerful, All-Loving God

The argument goes something like this: if God were all loving, He would not allow evil to exist. If God were all powerful, He could do away with evil. Since evil exists, God must not exist. Is this a good argument? Let's take a look. Since God is all loving, He does not force anyone to love Him. Love is self-sacrificing, not self-absorbed. Love gives of oneself. He allows people to not love Him. This is true love, the creation of a being that offers a relationship with open arms and complete forgiveness to His creation, human beings, but they are not forced to take the offer. What kind of love would it be if we were all forced to love God?

We cannot force other people to love us. It is not freedom, and it is not love. It is not love to hold a gun to a spouse's head and force him or her to say, "I love you." God is all loving because He made us and gave us the choice, and He respects our choice. Because we have the free choice to reject God and depend on our own understanding, we make wrong choices. As any child knows, wrong choices have consequences. People get hurt, and there is pain and suffering.

God is all powerful because He created time, space, and the cosmos. We owe Him nothing. He could extinguish the world as quickly as He spoke it into existence. However, He chooses not to. Through the most gracious and loving act ever demonstrated, God left His throne to come to earth to live among us as a human being to live a perfect life and then die a criminal's death. The question isn't how an all-powerful and all-loving God could exist in a world with evil but why we humans commit so much evil and not run toward and accept this free offer of grace and peace from such an all-loving and powerful God.

We know that God is all powerful and that this world may not currently be the best world as it is, but maybe this world is the best means to the greatest possible world. Just because evil exists right now doesn't mean it will always exist. God can and does deal with evil. God has dealt with evil in the past. In Genesis 6: 5-7, God contemplated wiping every person and every living creature off the earth.

> When the LORD saw that man's wickedness was widespread on the earth and that every scheme his mind thought of was nothing but evil all the time, the LORD regretted that He had made man on the earth, and He was grieved in His heart. Then the LORD said, "I will wipe off from the face of the earth mankind, whom I created, together with the animals, creatures that crawl, and birds of the sky— for I regret that I made them."

Whoever says God cannot and has not dealt with evil shows biblical ignorance. This is a clear example of God's righteous judgment on the earth at that time.

It is important to remember two more things about this. First, despite the extreme wickedness of these people, God gave them ample time to repent and ask for forgiveness before acting out His wraith. God did not just reflexively and quickly react to the evil in the world; He allowed Noah to build the huge ark in broad daylight in the midst of everyone. He proclaimed the Lord's words and provided plenty of warning. This is not a God who is rash and harsh with His people though it could be argued they deserved less mercy and warning.

Second, Genesis says God was grieved by this. He was not a bully. He regretted He had made humans. Man's wickedness was widespread, and every scheme in man's mind was nothing but evil all the time. Do we not all recognize evil when we see it? If there is no one to administer justice on earth since everyone was committing nothing but evil all the time, shouldn't it be up to God to administer that justice? Do we think God ought to have left things alone? Is it not up to God to decide if or when He wants to act out of His own righteous judgment or use other tools at His disposal?

Even after He destroyed His own creation, in His mercy, He allowed us to flourish again though He knew of our inclination for evil. In Genesis 8: 20-21, God promised to not destroy humankind again.

> Then Noah built an altar to the LORD. He took some of every kind of clean animal and every kind of clean bird and offered burnt offerings on the altar. When the LORD smelled the pleasing aroma, He said to Himself, "I will never again curse the ground because of man, even though man's inclination is evil from his youth. And I will never again strike down every living thing as I have done."

God is no bully. Anyone who claims the God of the Old Testament is a bully or homophobe is untutored and sophomoric. Name-calling is an uninformed, misguided, schoolyard tactic and straw-man strategy. Schoolyard tactics are identified easily and imply that those who utilize them have no good arguments of their own and undoubtedly don't understand the basics of what they are arguing against.

The Lord is merciful as well as patient. He entered our man-made suffering and experienced humiliation, pain, and death. We do not have a hands-off God who has left us alone to figure things out on our own; we have a God who acts.

The God of Happiness?

My pastor has made the point on occasion that the biblical God is not the God of happiness but rather the God of holiness. Atheist Richard Dawkins has described the God of the Old Testament in this way.

> The God of the Old Testament is arguably the most unpleasant character in all fiction: jealous and proud of it; a petty, unjust, unforgiving control-freak; a vindictive, bloodthirsty ethnic cleanser; a misogynistic, homophobic, racist, infanticidal, genocidal, filicidal, pestilential, megalomaniacal, sadomasochistic, capriciously malevolent bully. (Dawkins, The God Delusion, 2006)

That is clearly not the God Christians believe in; this is a misrepresentation of the main character of the Bible and the description of a person who clearly has caused some traumatic distress in someone's life. We could easily go through these descriptions of God he has given and biblically prove the ignorance of the descriptions, but we do not need to spend the time.

What do people want from God? Do we wish we were all just robots and drones that God made to love and worship Him? God could have done that. Do we wish God would have made us unable to make our own choices so no one would ever choose wrong or hurt anyone else? Do we wish God would have just made life easier so we could be happy all the time? That sounds nice, but is that really what a loving God would do?

Who would want a parent who gave them everything they wanted when they were growing up no matter how dangerous it was? Wouldn't we call that an irresponsible parent? A parent who allows us to do anything we want without boundaries is a careless and negligent parent. Sure, God wants us to be happy most of the time, but that is not His main goal; His main goal is to transform us into beings more like Him. He wants to make us holy.

Discomfort can lead to development of character. That is the goal. We want a parent who cares about us, not one who just wants us to be happy all the time. We know that happiness is temporary and that not everything that makes us happy is actually good for us.

Does God Cause Evil?

Another argument that the skeptic and atheist makes is that the Bible gives evidence that God is not all loving and moral because He causes evil to happen. But is that an accurate argument? Exodus contains references to Pharaoh hardening his own heart and references to God hardening Pharaoh's heart (Exodus 4:21, 7:3, 13, 14, 22; 8:15, 19, 32; 9:7, 12, 34, 35; 10:1, 20, 27; 13:15). The hardening of Pharaoh's heart has nothing to do with God creating moral evil. God can show mercy to whomever He chooses to show mercy and can harden someone's heart as well.

God showed mercy to Pharaoh, but Pharaoh hardened his heart and did not accept the Lord's compassion. In Isaiah 45:7, God said, "I form light and create darkness, I make success and create disaster; I Yahweh, do all these things." The Hebrew word for disaster is *ra'* or *raw-aw'*, affliction,

KRIS F. FRENCH, MD

calamity, distress, disaster, or evil (Strong, 2007). We know from the whole context of the Bible that God does not and did not create evil but does allow or bring about disaster, distress, and affliction.

We Christians have a worldview that allows us to maturely deal with suffering and affliction. In 2 Corinthians 4:8–9, Paul wrote, "We are pressured in every way, but not crushed; we are perplexed, but not in despair; we are persecuted, but not abandoned; we are struck down, but not destroyed." Later in 2 Corinthians 4:17–18, Paul wrote, "For our momentary light affliction is producing for us an absolutely incomparable eternal weight of glory. So we do not focus on what is seen, but on what is unseen. For what is seen is temporary, but what is unseen is eternal." In Matthew 24:9, Jesus said, "Then they will hand you over for persecution, and they will kill you. You will be hated by all nations because of My Name."

Only the Christian worldview gives us a complete understanding of suffering and affliction. We know that because this world is broken due to our sinful decisions, there will be pain and suffering. We know we will face afflictions, but we also know we can overcome them because Jesus did. No other worldview gives this complete picture of the problem of suffering and evil. God creates things that are good. Evil is the corruption of what has been created. We need to keep in mind that our view of good and bad, right and wrong, is limited by time and perspective and biased by our changing emotions. God, who is outside time, has the big picture view of all good and bad, right and wrong. We have no idea what He is doing with the badness people currently experience.

Differential Diagnosis

Atheism, theism, and polytheism offer solutions to the question of morality. Atheism says that morality is based on evolution and natural selection and that sociobiological conditioning has established the standards for what is right and wrong. Pluralism basically concludes that there really is no right or wrong. What is right for one person may be wrong for another. Good and bad are just illusory or else created by each person. Suffering is an illusion according to pluralism. The new-age creed "Create your own reality according to what feels right for you" means that anything you choose is "right" for you. This method of morality is a design-your-own ethics menu that allows you to choose from options based on personal preference. Fortunately, theism offers a complete view of morality given that there is a moral lawgiver.

Atheism	Theism
• Morals are cultural.	• Moral values are intrinsic to humans (physical objects do not possess moral values).
• Good or bad have to do with biochemical physical processes in the brain.	• A moral lawgiver set the standards for values and duties.
• Moral values are psychological constructs for which behaviors are determined by neurochemical processes.	• Humans have free will, intrinsic value, and worth.

The idea that good and bad or right and wrong are not real does not fit. We all know that if someone lies to us, we take offense. Morality is not an illusion. There are objective and corresponding values in reality. There must be a standard for setting the measuring line. The weight of the evidence places theism on the top of the differential diagnosis again.

The Physician's Conclusion

Patients do not let physicians off the hook with answers that may make sense to the physicians but not to them. Doctors cannot tell patients, "I believe you have MS because that's what it feels like to me." That makes no sense to the doctor or the patient. Pluralism doesn't fit with reality.

Atheism seems to do something similar; it offers people no satisfying answers to their medical conditions. Science offers people with explanations as to what genetic mutation occurred and the inflammatory cascade that ensued in the central nervous system causing the damage in a patient with MS, but science does not offer the why or the how. Atheism and naturalism do not offer that answer either. Patients are not content with an answer that says that it's all due to just chemistry and a misfire of atoms; that doesn't gratify their desire to know why this happened.

Without an ultimate purpose, there is no context for why things occur. It ultimately doesn't even matter. For example, when people say they lost loved ones to MS, what hope does the atheist have to offer them? That their lives make no difference in the long run?

Physicians know this when they use diagnostic criteria as well. Certain pieces of evidence are much more helpful at explaining things than others. When a person with known MS complains of new symptoms such as a dragging right foot, the neurologist will not lazily disregard the symptoms and blame it on MS. It may be due to MS, but other things can cause foot dragging as well. It could be due to a pinched spinal nerve or damage to another nerve. These things need to be evaluated for their worth in order to help the patient understand the what and the why. Atheism doesn't give us an appropriate how or why. Fortunately, theism does both.

The Atheist's Misdiagnosis

The atheist has no great explanation for why there is right and wrong. They can use schoolyard tactics to display their ignorance of theology, but they cannot honestly say Adolf Hitler was wrong in exterminating Jews and gypsies. They cannot even argue that the Crusades or the Salem witch hunts were wrong! By doing that, they are stating there is something wrong with that and evil exists. There are numerous atrocities recorded throughout history perpetrated in the name of religions, and that is clearly wrong. But the amount of suffering in the name of religion pales in comparison to the amount in the name of materialism, and that's in the twentieth century alone.

The worldview that says the health of society as a whole is so important that the weakest and incurable members of a society can or should be discarded and "granted a merciful death" is the ultimate implication of a world without God (Lifton, 1986). What is special at all about being human? According to naturalists, nothing. Karl Brandt was one of Adolf Hitler's personal physicians and played a critical role in the extermination procedures of the Jews. He was a pupil of Alfred Erich Hoche, a German psychiatrist and proponent of euthanasia who in his book *Allowing the Destruction of Life Unworthy of Life*, called for the killing of the developmentally disabled because they were "empty shells of human beings" (Hoche, 1920). This view of human beings leads to the utilitarian vision that killing some people is actually useful and that some people are considered disposable. This is simply the wrong worldview.

Cohort Study

When morality is evaluated in the context of a cohort study, it is clear that with God, the observation of objective moral values and duties is the most likely outcome. It is hard to argue that objective moral values and duties do not exist. If they do not exist, cohort 1 is not associated and God does not exist. But we know that objective morals exist. For example, surveys demonstrate that people across cultures agree that infidelity is wrong morally. That can't be a cultural trait since it is cross-cultural. There appears to be no evolutionary advantage to extramarital affairs as no one profits (including the children), so evolution does not explain why infidelity is wrong or why it exists to the extent it does. The existence of sin does explain it well. We are selfish and we crave pleasure no matter how fleeting the experience. Since we know objective morals exist, cohort 1 must be the best explanation for outcome 1. In fact, outcome 1 does not occur without God. Only outcome 2 can exist without God, but we know that outcome 2 is not reality. So God must be the causative association for outcome 1.

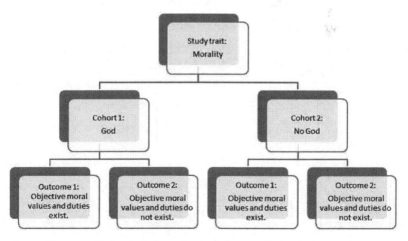

Figure 5: Cohort study evaluating the association between the observation of moral values and the existence of God

CHAPTER 7

Botox, Intestinal Bacteria, and Christianity's Coherent Creator

For as the body is one and has many parts, and all the parts of that body, though many, are one body—so also is Christ.

—1 Corinthians 12:12

You may be wondering what Botox and gut bacteria have to do with Christian apologetics. Like most people in America, in this day and age and with a little help from Hollywood, most of us are familiar with the cosmetic revolution that has taken place in plastic surgery and dermatology. However, many people are not aware of the medical use for and benefits of Botox. Furthermore, we are also quite familiar with TV commercials about probiotics and yogurt that provide "healthy" bacteria for our intestines.

We will spend a little bit of time reviewing some of the interesting and serendipitous history of Botox and some of the medical implications of gut bacteria. But before discussing botulinum toxin and gut bacteria, we will look at the argument of the interacting whole and how it relates.

The World as an Interacting Whole

As will be seen in later chapters, there are reasons to be amazed at the magnitude of the fine-tuned values for the existence of a habitable universe. Whether we believe it mere chance or that someone has chosen those particular values, they are astounding. In addition to our amazement of these facts, it is even more remarkable to think of how this whole system operates together.

William Norris Clark taught philosophy and metaphysics for years at Fordham University in New York. He developed an insightful argument for design using the idea of the universe as an interacting whole. Everything that exists seems to interact on some level at a specific ratio. The whole system cannot operate apart from the individual pieces, and the pieces cannot operate without each other. Peter Kreeft explained it this way.

In any system like our world, no component part or active element can be self-sufficient or self-explanatory. For any part presupposes all the other parts—the whole system already in place—to match its own relational properties. It can't act unless the others are there to interact reciprocally with it. (Kreeft, 1994)

This argument is compelling because the implication is that if the whole cannot exist without the parts nor the parts without the whole, neither can explain their existence and there must be some outside creator that designed it.

Poison to Medicine

Only in a world created by a merciful and creative God would the most toxic chemical known to us also be used to treat the suffering and debility associated with chronic pain. What a paradox! I would love to hear what Chesterton would have to say about this. Botulinum toxin is so potent that the equivalent of a quarter of the weight of a grain of sand (~350 nanograms) is a lethal human dose. This means that a little more than two pounds of it would be enough to kill the entire world population! Knowing this, who would ever agree to being treated with this protein?

Sausage Poisoning

It wasn't until the 1800s that it was discovered that botulinum toxin was produced by bacteria. Due to the poverty and decreased sanitary conditions as a result of the Napoleonic wars in Europe in the early 1800s, there were government warnings about contaminated food, and there were strict warnings about consumption of blood sausages. It wasn't until German medical officer Justinus Kerner's observations and descriptions that over a hundred cases were evaluated to be what is most consistent with food-borne botulism. His description of the symptoms including the progression of weakness and impaired gland secretion fits well with what is still known as the descending paralysis we see in current cases of botulism.

He investigated several possible causes of this poisoning and determined it must have been some sort of biological agent; he termed it "fat poisoning." He carried out many animal experiments and eventually even tried it himself with a very small amount on his tongue. He wrote, "Some drops of the acid brought onto the tongue cause great drying out of the mouth and the pharynx" (Truong, 2009).

After Kerner's experiments, it wasn't until approximately 1897 that it was finally discovered the poisoning was caused by a toxin produced by bacteria. German microbiologist Emile van Ermengem assisted in the autopsies of several people who had died in a food poisoning outbreak at a funeral in 1895. Van Ermengem discovered that a bacteria produced a toxin in low-oxygen conditions and termed the bacteria *Bacillus botulinus*. He concluded that the sausage poisoning and fat poisoning was not an infection but due to a toxic chemical produced by these bacteria (Truong, 2009). Since then, it has been shown that the main bacterial species that produces botulinum toxin is *Clostridium botulinum* and that there are at least eight known different toxins.

Clinical Application of Botulinum Toxin

In the late 1960s, intense investigation went into trying to see if botulinum toxin could be a biological weapon. The first batch of botulinum toxin used in clinical practice was for the treatment of strabismus (misaligned eyes due to muscle dysfunction). By the mid-1980s, botulinum toxin had been studied in the treatment of several neuromuscular disorders such as hemifacial spasm, strabismus, and cervical dystonia (all of which are disorders of muscles that cause spasming and facial disfigurement) (Truong, 2009).

Over the past twenty or thirty years, botulinum toxin has been used to treat bladder dysfunction, gastrointestinal dysfunction, pain disorders, and movement disorders. The botulinum toxin is considered a neurotoxin as it impairs signals from nerves to muscle. It's a protein that has two connected chains of amino acids. When the toxin is ingested or injected, it binds to proteins in nerves. The proteins function to help neurotransmitters in the nerve send signals to the muscles. Many of them are called docking proteins. The neurotransmitter is stored inside sacks in the nerves called vesicles. Proteins in nerves help the vesicles dock to the ends of the nerves to send the neurotransmitter out of the nerve, across the junction between the nerve and muscle, and then to the surface of the muscle, which then can allow the muscle to contract.

Botulinum toxin causes the loss of function of certain proteins making the acetylcholine vesicle unable to dock to the end of the nerve and release the neurotransmitter. Clinically, this results in the inability of the muscle to contract. In cases of botulism, paralysis occurs, but when it's used in certain ways as therapy, this results in a focused and targeted decrease in the flow of signals from the nerve to the muscle resulting in the desired effect. For example, cosmetically, botulinum toxin works to relax muscles and results in decreased wrinkles on the forehead or near the eyes; "crow's feet". Medically, it works to reduce the tone of muscle when tight muscles are causing dysfunction. For example, in cerebral palsy or multiple sclerosis, tight muscles are "relaxed" with botulinum toxin by decreasing the signal from the nerve to the muscle and this helps reduce the painful spasms of muscles and increases range of motion across their joints.

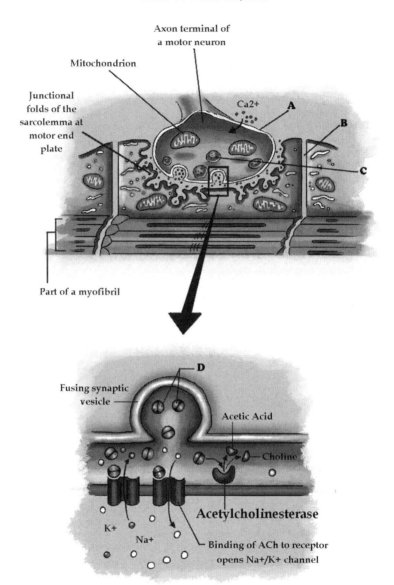

Axon terminal of
a motor neuron

Mitochondrion

Junctional
folds of the
sarcolemma at
motor end
plate

Ca2+   A

B

C

Part of a myofibril

D

Fusing synaptic
vesicle

Acetic Acid

Choline

Acetylcholinesterase

K+

Na+

Binding of ACh to receptor
opens Na+/K+ channel

Here's an illustration of the way botulinum toxin works. Picture a large
cruise ship with thousands of people. The cruise ship is the vesicle and the
people aboard are the neurotransmitters. The cruise ship wants to dock to
unload the people so they can buy souvenirs and drinks, so it needs help
from tugboats to get to the dock. Imagine torpedoes fired at the tugboats

that destroy them. The passengers can't get to the dock, so the island is left paralyzed—no one can buy souvenirs and beverages there.

Fortunately, the effects of botulinum toxin are temporary. The toxin is broken down over several weeks, but the effects last up to three to six months. The main reason the muscle effects last this long has to do with the irreversible damage it causes to the docking proteins. New proteins formed in the cell body are manufactured, but it takes months for them to travel down the nerve axon to the end where the neurotransmitter vesicles are.

Pain Reduction

Besides these effects on muscle tone, another critical clinical effect also takes place. This is the beneficial response that people report with pain reduction after getting botulinum toxin treatment. Botulinum toxin has been found to have dramatic reduction in certain pain disorders such as chronic migraines, phantom limb pain, and neck pain. The reason for this seems to be separate from its effects on the docking proteins. It seems to have an effect on pain neuropeptide signals released from certain nerves and other cells. For example, it seems to block or disrupt the signal of a pain chemical in the body called CGRP (calcitonin gene related peptide). There are several of these pain neuropeptides, but botulinum toxin seems to affect CGRP as well as another pain protein called substance P (Kim, 2015). By blocking these chemicals with botulinum toxin, the clinical result can be a dramatic reduction in chronic pain. In my clinical practice, this can further be translated into fewer missed workdays, less chronic suffering from pain, fewer visits to the ER, less pain medications, and an improved quality of life.

Eat Your Yogurt!

Let's move to another example of the cooperative interaction that exists in our daily lives. Our intestines are teeming with life that is not of ourselves. Yes, our bodies have approximately 10 trillion cells that collectively make up our physical bodies, but there coexists with us over

1,000 species of bacteria that live in and on us like their own planet, and they number approximately 30 trillion (three times the number of our own cells). We carry between three and six pounds of bacteria in our guts! That means that when we step on the scale, we can attribute roughly five pounds to creatures inside us (the gut flora).

Microbiome is a term for the amount and types of organisms that reside in our intestines and make up their own ecosystem. This is remarkable, but what's even more remarkable is the role these organisms play in our existence. Extensive research in this field focuses on the bacteria and their genetic makeup. Great progress has been made over recent years in terms of culturing bacterial species and sequencing RNA and DNA (Schreiner, 2015).

The roles these bacteria play are being discovered though we have taken them for granted. Most people are aware that they have bacteria in their intestines. We know that taking antibiotics can disrupt the normal function of the intestines leading to diarrhea or constipation. Most people are aware of the usefulness of consuming products with live bacteria such as yogurt to help restore the gut flora, that is, the bacteria and other living things in the gut. If the gut flora is not restored, disease-causing bacteria can take over and cause problems such as *C. difficile* colitis. If untreated, the overcolonization of harmful bacteria can lead to death. So it is necessary to have a diverse collection of bacteria and other microbes in our intestines.

Just as in the world of politics, our intestines cannot survive tyrannical bacteria. It has been demonstrated that diet affects which overall type of bacteria resides in the intestine—more pro-inflammatory versus anti-inflammatory bacteria.

Not so Fast, Germophobes!

The amount and diversity of bacteria in our guts have roles to play in our organ system management as well. Disruption of the balance of the gut microbes can affect the gastrointestinal system and cause systemic and diffuse effects in the immune and cardiovascular systems (Forbes, 2016). These microbes metabolize the formation of short-chain fatty acids from dietary fiber our bodies can't break down. These short-chain fatty acids are critical for energy generation as well as immune system signaling (Schreiner, 2015). Colon cancer tumor genesis responds to certain short-chain fatty acids produced by gut bacteria.

Furthermore, the immune system is highly responsive and dependent on the bacteria in our gastrointestinal system. The bacteria in the gut "talk" to our immune system and educate each other on foreign pathogen defense as well as overall anti-inflammatory and pro-inflammatory balance. There is growing interest also in the role that the gut microbiome plays in the overall health of the cardiovascular system. Trimethylamine-N-oxide (TMAO), a metabolite generated by bacteria in the gut, is associated with the formation of atherosclerosis in the blood vessels that can lead to heart attack and stroke (Schreiner, 2015). People who maintain vegan diets tend to have lower levels of TMAO and a lower risk of developing heart disease and stroke.

The microbial community in the intestines also plays an important role in keeping the central nervous system healthy. We know the immune system patrols and monitors the health of the brain. Interestingly, bacteria in the gut can produce certain proteins that help the immune system protect the CNS from pathogens and other pro-inflammatory attacks (Forbes, 2016).

Cooperative Uniformity of Creation

In a world with difficult questions about why we suffer and have to deal with evil, for some reason, we have chemicals such as botulinum toxin and have 30 trillion bacteria living in our guts. Think about botulinum toxin, the deadliest chemical known to us that can incredibly be used to decrease suffering and pain. The world seems to act in an interlocking manner with pieces that cause detriment in one fashion but create restoration in another. This establishes coherency between the interacting whole of the universe and God's role in it.

We humans have introduced sin and pain, but He offers relief. A toxic protein from a bacterial spore dating back to ancient, prehuman earth is being used to improve human functioning and decrease human suffering. Multiple deaths from botulism have over time unlocked the mysteries of the therapeutic benefit of this poison. The remarkable preservation of this toxin is mystifying. What was the toxin produced for in the first place? It seems that it has had a purpose planned for it throughout the centuries.

Norris Clark has formulated the theory of the interacting whole as an argument for a transcendent creator. The idea of such interacting parts that can create chaos or relief is unimaginable. Natural selection does not account for the cooperative nature of the botulinum toxin. According to natural selection, it was made to protect and preserve the bacterial spores. But now, humans are mass-producing botulinum toxin to treat diseases. The most toxic and deadly chemical in existence is used to treat incurable disorders and reduce pain. Evolution does not explain the paradoxes in this world. The cooperative uniformity of creation is obvious.

Blessings and Curses

The use of botulinum toxin is not the same as using chemo to treat cancer. Chemotherapies are synthetic drugs that interfere with the disease. Botulinum toxin is manufactured in the bacteria to help preserve the spore. The bacteria have been created by God, but their disease-producing proteins were not meant for suffering and pain. This cooperative uniformity is further established in the presence of such a diverse and amazing ecosystem that has been discovered in our guts. The bacteria help break down what we consume, they protect us from bad things that we consume (*E. coli*–infested burritos), they create signals to balance our immune system function, and they produce proteins that can protect us against cardiovascular disease.

Even when we annihilate their whole existence with our powerful antimicrobials, they come back and help us. Even when we oversanitize our kids and our homes, they keep us safe from other harmful microbes. As human beings, we do not understand very well that our existence is completely dependent on uncontrollable factors. The paradox is that we have developed such a profound fear of sickness and illness that we are destroying our own existence by antibiotically eradicating our life-sustaining microbiome.

Antibiotic abuse has created such a problematic resistance that we can nearly guarantee hospital-acquired infections for certain populations of people. The oversanitization that parents shower their children with to supposedly protect them from germs may very well have led to the super-hygienic society we live in with autoimmune disorders rampant among us. The question "Why does God allow MS?" may best be answered by the fact that God gave us a healthy gut microbiome, but in our own misguided understandings, we have demolished them with the blessing of penicillin and hand sanitizers. It is no wonder that without wisdom, a blessing can become a curse. I must clarify here that it is not the direct result of the use of hand sanitizers and hygiene that has manifested autoimmune disorders. As has been stated previously, rarely is there ever a single factor that is necessary or sufficient by itself to cause anything. But, environmental exposures play a role and we do not have all of the information as to the degree in which our intentions may have some harmful consequences.

Innovative Cohesion of Reality

As we have seen previously, God does not create evil. God is creative and innovative in His design, and He created us in His image with innovative abilities. God designed/created reality, and in our human free agency, we have altered the perfect creation and allowed disease to enter. Since God is all knowing, He can allow evil/disease/suffering for a reason we do not know or understand. This is analogous to a father allowing his children to undergo the pain of vaccination to prevent disease later. No matter how much the greater good is explained to the children, they still would rather not have the shots! Since God is all powerful, He can use anything in creation for our good (treatment of pain). Since He is creative, He gives us the ability to discover His creation and the treatments it offers. Since He is all loving, He gives us the treatment for the pain and suffering we have created. The coherence of the universe as an interacting whole and God's role in it shows us His mercy. We humans botch up His design and creation. He gives us Botox. I can only imagine how much this infuriates the devil!

Differential Diagnosis

Atheism	Theism
• Botulinum toxin exists only to preserve the bacteria.	• Botulinum toxin and gut bacteria act as parts of an interacting whole in a cooperative fashion.
• 1,000 species of bacteria live off us and control our immune system.	

The Physician's Conclusion

This universe seems to have a cooperative interaction to it just as medicine does. There seems to be a hand involved that helps unlock its mysteries. The fact that humans can learn to utilize such substances and consider the possibility of treatment seems to lead to the idea that humans are unique. We are unique in ways other than just the size of our brains compared to primates.

An evolutionary instinct would be to avoid a toxic chemical. Evolutionarily, it would be stupid to attempt to use such a toxic chemical and expose people to it. Thanks to God, we have our creative and adventurous minds to investigate the amazing world He has created. Medicine requires creativity and investigation to explore treatment potentials.

No treatment for a disorder is by itself complete or satisfactory without including the whole picture of the patient. Holistic treatment that includes immune modulatory medications is used to treat MS, but these medications are much more effective if they are coupled with lifestyle modifications including quitting smoking, vitamin D intake, low sodium consumption, exercise and fitness, and overall health management. No treatment should be considered effective in isolation.

The Atheist's Misdiagnosis

If it were up to the atheist and natural selection, we wouldn't have tried botulinum toxin as a therapy. But we have learned that the universe depends on its parts and the parts depend on the whole in an interlocking way. Without the whole, the parts don't work, and without the parts, the whole doesn't work. Something beyond the universe must exist. The atheist cannot explain how these parts interact with each other in such amazing and designed ways.

Cohort Study

Since the universe as a whole cannot explain or create itself nor can the individual components explain themselves, we must conclude an external explanation. Since all the components interact dependently in the universe and the universe cannot exist without its basic constituents, the universe must depend on its parts. The universe is not a sufficient explanation for why anything else exists.

The universe and everything in it interact as a whole, and it would take something outside the universe to cause it. The observation that a deadly protein such as botulinum toxin can interact in a human to reduce symptoms of pain and disease is not explainable by natural selection and macroevolution. How can natural selection account for the fact that a protective protein for *Clostridium botulinum* meant to destroy a predator can help treat severe pain and disability? Natural selection would do the opposite. It is not that humans have evolved the capability to respond positively to botulinum toxin. There has actually been nothing that evolved or was selected for to change the botulinum toxin or the proteins it affects in the motor nerves. It just happens that the botulinum toxin is beneficial for certain human disorders. It seems to be connected in some way.

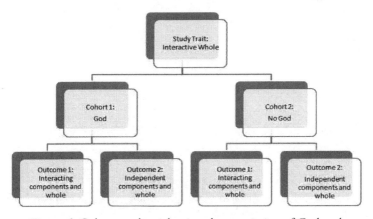

Figure 6. Cohort study evaluating the association of God and the outcome of interacting components and whole

In a similar way, the gut microbiome acts in an amazing way to talk to our immune systems to help or hinder us in this world. Why would that be the case based on evolution? Shouldn't we rely less on such simple creatures as one-celled organisms? How humbling it is that over 1,000 different species live on and in us and control much of the function of our major organ systems? It appears that all components of the universe have a connection and are involved in a grand scheme together. It appears that a grand author has written a play with all the actors coming together in cooperative uniformity. Without God, there is no explanation as to why everything works together. Outcome 1 is what we observe, and there are no parts in the universe that do not act on another part of it, so there are no exclusively independent components. Without an external, spaceless, and timeless cause, outcome 1 does not occur. But it is in fact outcome 1 that we observe. So cohort 1 must be the exposure cohort and God must be the cause.

CHAPTER 8

My Cousin the Cucumber

So God created man in His own image; He created him
in the image of God; He created them male and female.

–Genesis 1:27

Questioning Origins

I remember in undergraduate studies sitting in my evolution course trying
to make sense of it all. Descent with modifications through random genetic
mutations acted upon by a mysterious force of natural selection to create
the world as we see it. Genetic drift randomly affecting populations as well
as gene flow or migration creating the diversity in the genetic makeup of
populations. Mindless, unguided, mechanisms to explain why I'm sitting
in this course learning about this invisible force that made it possible for
me to understand them.

Where did life start, and how did consciousness begin? Do you want me
to believe once the correct chemical interactions came together—voilà—I
could think? I could make decisions? All because some unconscious matter
and chemicals interacting with each other, the first living thing "came to
life"? Can you imagine what that looked like? Did the first one die since
it wasn't able to reproduce? Or was there a sudden explosion of life at that
point and some were able to survive the conditions and replicate while

others couldn't? What process made a lifeless form of chemical soup be able to say, "I'm alive!"?

Does that really happen? Has anyone ever witnessed it? Has anyone seen a rock suddenly take a breath or a glass of water talk? John Locke stated, "It is as impossible to conceive that ever bare incogitative matter should produce a thinking, intelligent being, as that nothing should of itself produce matter." (Locke, 1689, pp. BookIV, Chapter10). Doesn't it make much more sense that purely material beings such as pillows do not make or transform into living, thinking beings? We know that's impossible, but for some reason, we are led to believe the other way around.

According to naturalism, we all came from that initial living being. Our grandfather (or grandmother) in the initial Garden of Eden of primordial soup. Just as in the biblical account, there was no sin or pain, but our ancient, single-celled ancestors survived, and here we are. Do you think that Ancestry.com can get us traced all the way back there so we can think of and picture our great grandparents? Or at least trace it back to when we diverged on the tree of life with vegetables so I break up the awkward silence at the dinner table with my cousin the cucumber?

Truth Suppression

What does it mean to say things are designed or appear designed? In the academic world, this can cause several emotional reactions including vitriol among naturalist proponents. Why is that? Sir Francis Crick, one of the codiscoverers of the double-helix structure of the DNA molecule stated, "Biologists must constantly keep in mind that what they see was not designed, but rather evolved" (Crick, 1990). Why do biologists need to "constantly keep this in mind"? The apostle Paul stated in Romans 1:18–19,

> For God's wrath is revealed from heaven against all the godlessness and unrighteousness of people who by their unrighteousness suppress the truth, since what can be known about God is evident among them, because God has shown it to them.

In this chapter, we will see that God has set up the parameters for life in a perfect balance. No physician looks at perfect balance and thinks there was no one involved in balancing it. We do not give chance that option. We will first look at the stars to examine some of the elements that have been programmed with such great precision from the beginning of time until today and zoom in closer into our own planetary conditions. And then finally and most important, we will look at the clear and obvious design of life in our bodies.

Finely Tuned for Existence

The term *fine-tuned* does not mean intelligent design; it refers to the different values impeccably set in order to allow this life-permitting universe. The precision of the fine-tuning constants and conditions is a noncontroversial topic; the explanation of the fine-tuning in the cosmos is what is deemed controversial. The idea of a fine-tuner is where the argument lies.

How is this world so perfectly conditioned to allow life to originate and be sustained? Teleology comes from the Greek *telos* (end, purpose, design). Telos is synonymous with the Latin version of *perfectus*, perfected. Teleology is a branch of philosophy that deals with the study of nature's purpose or design. There seems to be an order to everything. Plato in his Laws, wrote, "from the order of the motion of the stars and of all things under the dominion of the Mind which ordered the universe."

Scientists have assumed that with enough time and matter, life would by chance emerge. Astronomical evidence has demonstrated that this is just not the case. There seems to be such a fine balance between this "perfect" world existing to provide life and order and not existing at all. The scientific evidence actually leads to the probability that life would never emerge by chance. The number of atoms in the known universe is between 1×10^{78} and 1×10^{80}. According to astronomer Sir Frederick Hoyle, the chance of the approximately 2,000 proteins coming together by chance in a bacterium is $1 \times 10^{40,000}$. In other words, it is impossible.

The Copernican Principle

In the 1500s, Nicolas Copernicus was having a difficult time making sense of his mathematical calculations regarding the motion of the planets and stars with the geocentric model of the solar system. His hypothesis was finally that the sun must be at the center of the solar system and the earth seemed to rotate as well. This was contrary to what at the time seemed to be common sense that the earth seemed to be the center with everything in the heavens rotating around it. There was no notion of gravity at the time, so the idea of the earth rotating was also contrary to common sense. If the earth is rotating, why don't we land in a different place after we jump up?

It is important to note that Copernicus did not "demote" the earth; he didn't think the earth was any less special or significant not being at the center of the universe. This is an important point to be made since what has come from this idea is the notion of the principle of mediocrity, the idea that since the earth is not at the center of the universe, there is nothing special about it. It goes further than that. It states that earth is an ordinary planet circling an ordinary star in an ordinary galaxy in an ordinary universe.

Besides the ordinary nature of our planet and solar system, the location of our solar system in the Milky Way is also not special. Since it was discovered that our solar system is actually not at the center of the Milky Way, we are supposedly considered less special as well according to this principle. But when we start looking at all the scientific evidence in terms of the special conditions and qualities, the story changes. We learn that the earth is unique in multiple regards including the presence of the moon, the size of our moon, the nature of the sun, our location in the solar system, the presence of our neighborhood planets in the solar system, the type and size of the Milky Way, the location of our solar system in the Milky Way, the existence of the magnetosphere around the earth—on and on. The main question is whether the universe has any other life-permitting planets with these same characteristics. Does it take a fine-tuned universe to make a planet like earth habitable? The universe seems too large not to have more life, but maybe that's how large and complex it needs to be for there to be even one life-permitting planet such as earth.

The so-called fine-tuning of the necessary qualities and quantities of the initial conditions are staggering in that there cannot have been any different known conditions that would have resulted in such a perfect setting for the development of our existence. These settings fit into such a tight range of values that any change or disruption in any one of them would result in our nonexistence. Numerous examples of fine-tuning exist, many more than I have the knowledge or experience to explain. For better and more in-depth explanations, you can consult a great many resources including *The Teleological Argument: An exploration of the fine-tuning of the cosmos* in the *Blackwell Companion to Natural Theology* by William Lane Craig and J. P. Moreland, *The Road to Reality* by Roger Penrose, and *Just Six Numbers* by Martin Rees.

It is worth the effort to go into a discussion of some of them along with the reasoning behind why it is important to understand. But before we do that, let us understand what is meant by these constants and conditions. We can categorize the elements of the fine-tuning argument into these groups.

1. the four fundamental forces of nature
2. the cosmological constant
3. the initial cosmological conditions
4. the local conditions of our solar system and planet necessary for life

The four fundamental forces refer to the main four interaction forces of nature such as gravitation, the electromagnetic force, and the weak and strong nuclear forces. The cosmological constant is included as a constant but is not one of the four main fundamental forces of nature. The initial conditions of the universe are more arbitrary numbers and include values such as the velocity of light, the ratio of the mass of a neutron compared to a proton, the ratio of the mass of a proton compared to an electron, and the precise mass of the universe.

In terms of the local conditions in regard to our solar system and planet, there are too many necessary conditions to discuss in one book. But several of them include the right planetary mass, the location in the circumstellar habitable zone, our time in the habitable age, the location of our solar system in the Milky Way, and its type and size.

Stay in the Box

Science used to be considered as the philosophy of nature. Isaac Newton's work *Mathematical Principles of Natural Philosophy*, which was published in 1687, described the laws of motion and mechanics by scientific and mathematical methods. He was a scientist but rightly known at the time as a natural philosopher. The scientific method requires testing a hypothesis and interpreting the results, but science is not entirely objective. It has now become such a politically and socially involved realm considered by many to have all of the answers to all questions whether scientific or not.

Scientists have been elevated to the status of ancient, wise sages who can answer any question a human could have. Science is now considered a study of the natural and material and nothing outside that box. No matter if the evidence is leading to something beyond materialism, we must stop the search and find an explanation in the box. Do not look outside the box!

Even if we perceive design in this universe, we are told evolution is the scientific answer to the appearance of design. Darwinists have done a good job at selling their ideas, and they have done a good job at selling the idea that intelligent design is not a branch of science. Intelligent design (ID) is basically a field of science that looks for evidence of design in nature. Intelligent design is not creationism no matter what professors or high school teachers may tell students.

Sean McDowell stated, "The most effective method for teaching naturalism is Darwinian evolution" (Dembski W. a., 2008). Unknown to most people, there are many secular scientists who are ID researchers, and there are nearly 100 peer-reviewed articles in scientific literature on the significance of ID as of December 2015. (For an updated account of the growing accumulation of scientific literature on ID, the Discovery Institute at www.discovery.org keeps a record of this information that is a priceless resource for a variety of cultural and scientific data and material.)

Evidence versus Proof

Some things are quite improbable but obviously not impossible. J. Warner Wallace states, "And that's the difference between evidence and proof. We can offer evidence all day long: facts about eyewitness testimony, archeological verification, and scientific harmony, but none of this will serve as proof unless God first changes a heart." (Wallace, 2013). Evidence is objective, but proof seems to depend on the person's own filters and biases that form his or her conclusions on a subject. The question is whether we need to draw a line somewhere and say that the probability of an event occurring by chance is so low that we can't consider it possible. William Dembski has come up with an idea of eliminating chance with small enough probabilities (Dembski W., 1998). Based on the estimation of the total number of atoms in the universe (1 x 10^{80}), the total number of seconds since the big bang (4 x 10^{17}), and the Planck time (1 x 10^{-43}), the probability that the universe was generated by chance from nonliving matter is roughly 1 in 10^{150} (Dembski W., 1998).

Fathom This

Some of the values of the variation in these numbers are so low that it is not even fathomable. We cannot understand what 1 x 10^{80} of anything is. It is currently estimated that there are approximately 1 x 10^{80} atoms in the universe (that's 10 with 80 zeros after it!). We can barely conceive 1 billion let alone 1 trillion or 1 billion trillion. An example of how difficult it is to fathom these numbers is given by Dr. William Lane Craig: "Having an accuracy of even one part in 10^{60} is like firing a bullet toward the other side of the observable universe, twenty billion light years away, and nailing a one-inch target!" (Craig, On Guard; Defending your faith with reason and precision, 2010).

There are many examples of hypothetical variations in the parameters of the universe and solar system that would change the ability of life formation. We will discuss only a few of these in this chapter. The goal is not to exhaust the list but to illustrate the idea and come up with reasons and the best explanation(s) for these fixed values. Is it possible that the values are due to chance? Is it probable? Is it probable that the values have been set by someone or something? Which makes the most sense with the data we have?

The Four Dimensionless Constants

The four fundamental forces of nature interact with each other and are not necessarily independent of each other. A small change in any one of them in the positive or the negative would increase the improbability of life formation in this universe.

1. The strong nuclear force, the most powerful of these four forces, refers to the interaction that holds the nuclei between atoms together. But atoms often repel each other because of the force of electromagnetism. Ultimately, the strong force must overcome this. If this were any weaker, the universe would have less of the stable chemicals necessary for the formation of amino acids, DNA, RNA, etc.
2. The weak nuclear force is the interaction between the most elementary particles that make up an atom such as fermions that include quarks and leptons. This force is involved in and responsible for radioactive decay and nuclear fission. Without its precise balanced strength, stars could not form.
3. Electromagnetism has to do with the force that holds an atom's nucleus together and has a repellant force with other atoms. Without the precision of the strength of this force, chemical bonds would not be stable enough to support life.
4. Finally, the gravitational constant is related to the influence of gravity, the attractive force between two body masses. If it were weaker, planets and stars could not form.

The Cosmological Constant

The discovery of this force is somewhat serendipitous and interesting. This force was initially hypothesized by Albert Einstein around 1917 to fit with his theory of general relativity when applied to the cosmos. At the time, like most people, Einstein thought that the universe was static and not expanding or contracting. His theory required a cosmological constant in addition to the theory of general relativity for him to obtain the calculations in accord with a static universe.

However, in 1929, when Edwin Hubble discovered that galaxies outside our group of galaxies were moving away from each other, he abandoned the theory of the constant. Einstein and all other cosmologists were surprised by the discovery that the universe was expanding and his cosmological constant did not seem to work with his general theory of relativity.

It was not until the 1990s with the advent of new technology that it was discovered the universe was accelerating in its expansion. This has been associated with the idea that most of the mass in the universe is made up of so-called dark energy, which dilutes slowly compared to "normal" matter.

Remarkably, the cosmological constant is consistent with the idea of dark matter. It can be expressed as a numerical value that controls the speed at which the universe is expanding. It is basically a hypothesized repulsive force to balance the gravitational forces in the universe. It is exquisitely fine-tuned to 1×10^{-120}; if it were marginally increased or decreased, the universe would either explode or contract (Ross, 1995).

Not only are all of the constants finely tuned in a narrow range of values, but the ratios of the constants are also related to each other. Each of these constants is dependent on the other, and if one is slightly changed, the others do not work. What are the chances that each one of these constants would find the value it currently has in order that the other constants would "cooperate" appropriately in order for life to exist? The chance is practically zero. Now what are the chances that one of the constants would match perfectly the value that needs to be met in order for another constant to work perfectly? Even closer to zero.

One specific example is the ratio of the number of protons to the number of electrons in the universe. If the ratio were higher, electromagnetism would dominate gravity and there would be no galaxy formation (Rees, 2000). For example, the maximum deviation for the ratio of the difference between the electromagnetic force and that of gravity is 1×10^{-40}. This number is not even fathomable. Dr. Hugh Ross gives an example of this in his book *The Creator and the Cosmos*.

One part in 10^{37} is such an incredibly sensitive balance that it is hard to visualize. The following analogy might help: Cover the entire North American continent in dimes all the way up to the moon a height of about 239,000 miles. Next, pile dimes from here to the moon on a billion other continents the same size as North America. Paint one dime red and mix it into the billions of piles of dimes. Blindfold a friend and ask him to pick out one dime. The odds that he will pick the red dime are one in 10^{37} (Ross, 1995)

This is such an improbability that any reasonable person would consider it impossible. We know that some things are highly improbable but not impossible. But to believe something, we need to use the evidence we have to make reasonable conclusions. When scientists speculate on theoretical conditions and the existence of multiuniverses, this is not consistent with the current evidence; it is speculative science and based on metaphysical philosophy rather than observation and reason.

Initial Conditions

But there are more reasons to believe that chance alone has not produced these unlikely events. The highly ordered initial state of the universe is so improbable by chance that the estimate of chance to produce that state is calculated at 1 in $10^{10(123)}$ (Penrose, 2004). These numbers are so embarrassingly small that it is hard not to sigh and roll our eyes. Example after example of all these values demonstrate repeatedly the improbability of time and chance resulting in the formation of anything let alone carbon-based life that can interact with the universe. But naturalists continue to say, "C'mon, give chance a chance!" As we will see, the complete unreasonableness of the idea of chance resulting in the formation of chemistry and life gets even worse for the naturalist as we begin to look at other conditions that are unique in order for our existence.

The Milky Way

Our place in the universe also plays a role in the ability for life to exist. The Milky Way is not a large galaxy or a very old galaxy; it is just the right age for our solar system to exist. Furthermore, the location of our central star and solar system seems just right as well for protection against the more hostile energy at the center of this galaxy.

Our solar system is between two of the spiral arms of the Milky Way—the Perseus arm on the outside and the Sagittarius arm on the inside. Since we are between the two arms and not in one, we are able to observe the Milky Way along with other galaxies. We seem to have a much clearer view not obscured by the extra galactic debris that would be in the way if we were in one of the arms. For example, on a clear night, it is actually possible to view with the naked eye Andromeda, our closest neighbor galaxy. If you can believe it, Andromeda is 2.5 million light years away.

For those not familiar with the idea of a light year, it's the distance light travels in one earth year. Since the velocity of light is 186,000 miles per second, light travels approximately 5.8 trillion miles in one year. And Andromeda is 2.5 million light years away! But we are still able to observe it from our backyards on a clear night. Talk about observability. If we were in one of the spiral arms, the chance of being able to view and study the cosmos as we can would be much less.

Goldilocks and Jupiter

Several more specifications for the development of life in the universe are more local to us. For example, we are at a perfect place in our solar system. Earth is in what astronomers call the Goldilocks zone. We are not too far from the sun or too close to it but just right. Furthermore, the mass of the earth is perfect for revolution around the sun, and the size of the moon is just right for its revolution around earth.

The anthropic (compatibility of the universe with life) principle proponent might say these things exist because we are here to observe them, but that does not let anyone off the hook as to why all these parameters are so perfect. There isn't one thing that is just a little off. Without the huge planet, Jupiter, earth may have been struck many more times by asteroids and we may not be here. Frank Turek said, "Thank God for Jupiter!" The great gas giants of our solar system like Jupiter help shield the earth from asteroids and comets. For example, the comet Shoemaker Levy-9 had been revolving around the sun but was caught up in Jupiter's powerful gravitational pull in the 1960s and ended up breaking apart in 1992. It collided with Jupiter in 1994 in dramatic fashion, and we were able to witness the event. For many reasons, Jupiter is referred to as the cosmic liver.

There is also some evidence that Jupiter is responsible for our oceans here on earth. Some people have labeled Jupiter as our Great Protector (Rasio, 1996). There are many more examples of these boundary parameters for the ability of a habitable universe to exist, so let's move closer to home.

Our Wonderful Moon

Astronomers agree that the old idea of the moon having "budded" off the earth 4 billion years ago when the earth was rotating much faster is no longer reasonable. Also, there is no reason to believe the moon was floating by and then captured by the earth's gravitational field.

Another idea is that a small planet collided with the earth over 4 billion years ago creating a ring of debris orbiting the earth that eventually turned into the moon (Comins, 1993). This seems to be the best explanation and theory since the moon is so large and perfectly round.

The liquid metal core in the earth seems to fit this idea. Our moon is a gift to us on earth, but most of us have taken it for granted. Without the moon, we wouldn't have the wonderful songs and poems that have been written about it. We wouldn't have the famous picture of E.T. flying in front of the moon or Tom Hanks standing in front of the gigantic moon on his midoceanic raft in *Joe Versus the Volcano*.

Besides those great aspects, our moon is actually considered necessary for our existence. It has slowed down the fast rotation of the earth so we can live without such wind speeds that we could not live here and the erosion of land and crops would not allow for life to exist. The moon stabilizes the axial tilt of the earth so our earth is much more constant in its angle and its axial rotation (Gonzalez, 2004).

Besides these amazing qualifications for life that the moon plays a part in, it also has allowed for the scientific discovery of many findings. For example, the ability for us to view a total eclipse of the sun is not offered on any other planet in our solar system. Actually, one of Saturn's moons, Prometheus, does offer a total solar eclipse, but it lasts less than a second. The total eclipse of the sun by Prometheus is also not a perfect eclipse because its shape is more like a potato and elongated, which does not allow for the perfect view of the sun's chromosphere around the edge of our moon (Gonzalez, 2004).

Our moon has allowed the visualization and study of the outer layer of the sun, the visible portion of light that we see around the moon during a total eclipse. Because of this, astronomers and physicists have been able to verify Einstein's theory of general relativity as light is bent by gravity. Total solar eclipses have allowed for the discovery of the genesis of stars, which has led to major scientific discoveries. As humans, we exist at what seems to be a perfect place and time in the cosmos. For example, we know that the moon is moving away from the earth at the rate of about 1.6 inches per year and in several million years, we will not have total and perfect solar eclipses. Moreover, the sun is about 400 times larger than the moon but the sun is 400 times farther from earth as the moon is, which makes the total solar eclipse possible for us to view at this time and from this place (Gonzalez, 2004). Is it just a coincidence that we have been placed on the planet earth at just the right time to be able to see total eclipses and make these scientific discoveries?

Perfect Earth

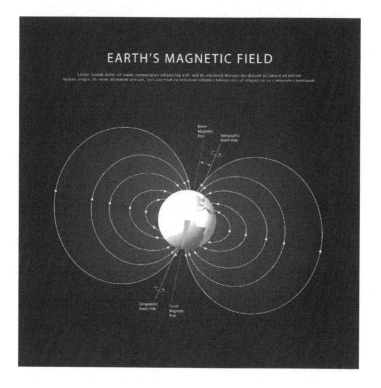

The earth is the densest planet in the solar system. This is in relation to the liquid iron and nickel core that circulates and creates the magnetosphere surrounding earth. The magnetosphere helps our compasses work correctly and protects the earth from the solar wind shooting out from our sun into the solar system. The liquid iron core circulates with the help of other features of this planet. Earth has a very thin crust—on average around four kilometers thick—that allows for plate tectonics to occur. With the ability of the crust to move appropriately, this creates the ability of the mantle to move and the iron core to circulate and create the magnetosphere (Gonzalez, 2004).

Perfect Size in the Universe

When we consider the vastness of the cosmos, we seem so small and meaningless in comparison. Since the heliocentric model of the solar system changed our view of the heavens, there has been a shift in the naturalist's goal to demonstrate how ordinary we are—not only our ordinariness but also that of our place in the solar system and Milky Way. But we forget that just because we are quite small compared to the cosmos, we are quite large compared to the quantum world. As humans, we are in fact near the mean in terms of logarithmic size compared to everything in the known universe. On a logarithmic scale with humans at a size designated 10^0, the diameter of the observable universe would be approximately 10^{26} whereas the size of quarks (the smallest known objects) is 10^{-20} (Gonzalez, 2004). We are actually optimum in terms of our size for the discoverability of the large-scale universe in addition to the extremes of the small-scale, quantum world.

Fine-Tuning Argument for Design

The numbers and values discussed so far are difficult to imagine, but they do not do anything to lead us to conclude they were set that way by God. Nor does the sheer existence of these values do anything to say that the anthropic principle is a good explanation. The low probability of the universe and then galaxies forming, the production and place of our solar system, earth as a planet with an atmosphere that allows the habitability of plants and animals, and the ability of sustenance from the sun to support and replenish life is difficult to imagine coming by chance alone, but it is not impossible. A logical argument developed by Craig is as follows (Craig, On Guard; Defending your faith with reason and precision, 2010).

1. The fine-tuning of the universe is due either to physical necessity, chance, or design.
2. It is not due to chance or physical necessity.
3. Therefore, it is due to design.

There doesn't seem to be another possible explanation to add to the first premise, and so the only two possible premises to object to are the second and the third. According to physical necessity, the values and constants have to have the values they do for life to exist in the universe. The so-called anthropic principle claims we are here to observe the universe and its physical laws because the constants and laws of nature exist as they do. But that does nothing to help us explain why they exist in such a delicate balance. All it does is make the observation without explaining the observation. There is no evidence that they must have the values they do. There may be another universe that has different values.

Second, as we have seen from the low probability of the particular set of values we have in this universe, the chance of one of them achieving the exact value that it has is low not to mention two of them or more. Dr. Craig gives a good example by bringing up the idea of

> a lottery in which billions and billions and billions of white ping-pong balls were mixed together with just one black ping-pong ball, and you were told that one ball will be randomly selected out of the horde. If it's black, you'll be allowed to live; if it's white, you'll be shot. No matter which ball rolls down the chute, the odds against the black ball are fantastically improbable. The crucial point is that whichever ball rolls down the chute, it is overwhelmingly more probable that it will be white rather than black. So, if the black ball rolls down the chute, you certainly should suspect that the lottery was rigged to let you live. (Craig, On Guard; Defending your faith with reason and precision, 2010)

Based on the low probability of this universe coming into existence by sheer chance, it seems that the best explanation is that the universe has a purpose and that there is a set value to things for some reason. There must be someone or something that set those values with a purpose in mind. The fact that the values are so exquisitely set and the fact we are here to observe and measure them points to intentionality.

Design in Biology

Let's change gears and now focus on the design here on earth. Before the discovery of the double helix of DNA in 1953 by geneticists James Watson and Francis Crick and the ability to "see" inside a cell, the biology of cells was considered not all that impressive. When the findings of the molecular machinery were revealed, the question of how and why became loud. Antony Flew was a devout atheist and British philosopher who spent his life defending the atheist belief system. In 2003, he was a contributing signer of the Humanist Manifesto III, but in 2004, after deeper investigations into DNA, cellular mechanisms, and cosmological fine-tuning, he renounced naturalism and became a deist.

When the search for truth leads us where we don't want to go, we must decide to follow it regardless of the consequences or suppress the truth and go our own ways. Discoveries in cell biology and biochemistry have set off a cascade of searching for where these processes come from. Can natural selection explain the protein functions in the cell? We shall find out.

Primer in DNA Transcription and Translation

DNA replication

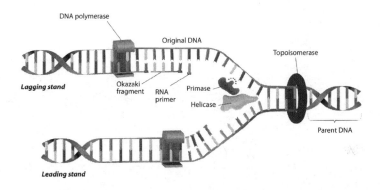

Any discussion of amino acids, proteins, DNA, and RNA can be abstract and confusing. Whether you are a trained geneticist or someone who has never studied or reviewed genetics or biochemistry, it is always wise to review the basics. Let us briefly discuss what these molecules are and where they come from. DNA is the code for basic information in the nucleus of the cell; it contains the genetic instructions for building proteins. It is made up of four different nucleotides bound in a chain that create a particular structure of the DNA molecule called the sugar-phosphate backbone.

The four nucleotides that make up the chain in DNA are cytosine

(C), guanine (G), adenine (A), and thymine (T). Each chain is bound to another to form the double-helix structure of DNA. The two strands of DNA carry the same information but run in directions opposite to each other. For them to bind properly, the nucleic acids can bind only to certain other nucleic acids resulting in base pairs; for example, A binds only to T and G only to C. When DNA is compacted in the nucleus, it is termed a chromosome. Humans have twenty-three pairs of chromosomes made up of DNA. The largest chromosome, chromosome 1, is made up of approximately 220 million base pairs.

A gene is a region of DNA that encodes a protein. The reading of DNA results in protein generation during a process called transcription. Each DNA chain is mechanically unbound from the other, and transcription protein machinery will read along the DNA sequences that it is programmed to and then go on to transcribe the DNA sequences into another smaller macromolecule called messenger RNA (mRNA).

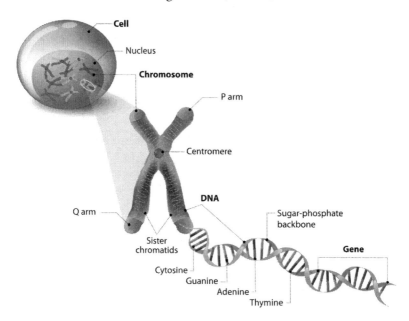

The mRNA is then usually directed out of the nucleus and has to undergo another process of decoding before a protein is generated. The process of decoding mRNA into amino acids is termed *translation*. But it is not that simple. The mRNA macromolecule must be directed out of the nucleus to a different location called the ribosome.

Interestingly, on a brief but related note, a ribosome is a large protein that translates mRNA into a chain of amino acids, so a ribosome must exist in order for a ribosome to be formed. Once the mRNA is in the ribosome, it is read by the ribosome and the corresponding amino acids are linked while other helping proteins fold and shape the amino acids into a functional protein. There are twenty standard amino acids each represented by a codon. A codon is a fundamental unit of DNA. Each codon is made up of a sequence of three nucleotides that together code for a specific amino acid or a signal to proteins to stop reading. The codon of the RNA that is read by the ribosome will code for a specific amino acid in that location of the protein chain.

The above is a very simplified version of these processes as they are beyond complex and the proteins are very specific in their jobs and duties. The reader can refer to biochemistry textbooks or online resources for more-detailed information.

Evolution's Problem

An obvious problem arises for the naturalist when we consider proteins, DNA, and RNA— which of these three molecules came first? As we had discussed earlier in the argument of the interacting whole, each of these molecules seems to require the other for function. For example, amino acids can potentially come together, but under what code and by what sequence are they organizing?

A simple nucleic acid chain of DNA may have evolved or formed out of the soup, but there are no proteins to decode and then transcribe it since DNA encodes those proteins. It gets no easier for RNA either since it usually comes from DNA in humans and is translated into proteins. There are certain things that exist that have only RNA and no DNA such as certain viruses, but the same problem continues. Did the RNA come about first? How did it replicate? How did it get decoded since we know RNA requires proteins to translate it? How did the first protein form from it?

Many evolutionists point to the RNA world hypothesis as evidence for which came first. But there still seems to be too many holes including the fact that we know DNA is transcribed to RNA and then RNA into protein. There is no evidence that it goes the other way. RNA is not stable by itself, and there is no evidence it is able to self-replicate. There is also the problem with how we went from an RNA world to the DNA and protein world we live in.

As if we hadn't reviewed enough evidence for the existence of a designer, let's now take a closer look at some of the recent scientific research into the biochemistry of design.

Examples of ID Research

As we have seen with many of the arguments for the existence of a creator and a designer, we have continued to experience the depth that this information goes. With the growing research into ID in the fields of biology, informatics, biochemistry, and physics, the case for design in nature becomes more complete. Many ID researchers agree that there must be some designer or guider of the processes we see. Laurence A. Cole has studied human brain growth and concluded that an intelligent agent must be behind the process. Studying the hormone human chorionic gonadotropin, he has concluded that the glycosylation (addition of a sugar to the protein after translation) of this molecule has evolved over time to allow for increased nutrition to a growing baby during pregnancy and consequently into the full human brain (Cole, 2015). He states,

> The odds of a mutation in the chorionic gonadotropin (CG) gene leading to increased CG biological activity may be very small, perhaps 1 in 1000 or 1 in 10,000 offspring. It appears that four mutations in the CG gene leading to major improvement in brain size occurred in a row. This progression occurred in a series in the pro-simian primate, lower simian primate, advanced simian primate, early hominid, and humanoids. Four of the 1 in 1000 or 1 in 10,0000 events occurring in a row appears like planned evolution rather than Darwinian evolution with remote odds of anywhere between 1 in a trillion and 1 in 10 quadrillion. (Cole, 2015)

Whether a person accepts the idea of guided evolution or theistic evolution, this research demonstrates that there must be some intelligence behind what we are seeing. The research points to a designer.

Irreducible Complexity

Since 1996, the battle between Darwinian evolution and ID has gone full force. One big reason the controversy has exploded is due to the brilliant discovery of a severe challenge for Darwin. Michael Behe, a biochemist at Lehigh University, performs biochemical research and has focused on Darwin's acknowledgment that there are certain things that if discovered would go against his theories: "If it could be demonstrated that any complex organ existed, which could not possibly have been formed by numerous, successive, slight modifications, my theory would absolutely break down" (Darwin, 1859).

Behe's concept of irreducible complexity has done just that.

An irreducibly complex system cannot be produced directly [that is, by continuously improving the initial function, which continues to work by the same mechanism] by slight, successive modifications of a precursor system, because any precursor to an irreducibly complex system that is missing a part is by definition nonfunctional. (Behe, Darwin's Black Box, 1996)

He has received tremendous unwarranted criticism since then, but the concept remains. There are so many examples of irreducible complexity in biology that it is almost unfair to the evolutionists. Behe wrote,

I argued that purposeful intelligent design, rather than Darwinian natural selection, better explains some aspects of the complexity that modern science has discovered at the molecular foundation of life. (Behe, Reply to My Critics: A Response to Reviews of Darwin's Black Box: The Biochemical Challenge to Evolution, 2001)

Despite the criticisms, many of the critics succumb to the lack of evidence that Darwinism offers. For example, evolutionary biologist Andrew Pomiankowski stated,

Pick up any biochemistry textbook, and you will find perhaps two or three references to evolution. Turn to one of these and you will be lucky to find anything better than "evolution selects the fittest molecules for their biological function." (Behe, Reply to My Critics: A Response to Reviews of Darwin's Black Box: The Biochemical Challenge to Evolution, 2001)

Kenneth Miller, a cell biologist at Brown University, stated in his book *Finding Darwin's God* that a true acid test of Darwinism's ability to generate systems with irreducible complexity would be to "use the tools of molecular genetics to wipe out an existing multipart system and then see if evolution can come to the rescue with a system to replace it." (Miller, 2007) Behe agrees that would be a great way to see if Darwinian evolution could handle this task. Miller directs us to the experiment of the *E. coli* lactose system. In this system, the sugar, lactose, causes the enzyme that breaks it down to turn on. It acts as an enzyme inducer for its own metabolism. The presence of lactose promotes expression of a certain portion of the bacterial DNA termed the lac operon. The lac operon codes for three proteins involved in lactose metabolism. The more lactose there is, the more the enzyme that breaks it down will be activated.

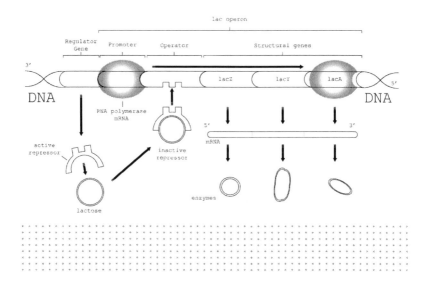

One of the three proteins encoded by the lac operon is galactosidase, which breaks down lactose. And it is known that the system does not work well without galactosidase. So in the experiment conducted by Miller, galactosidase is knocked out and the system does not operate as well. Wait a second! Doesn't that just demonstrate irreducible complexity?

Also, only one component of the whole experiment was wiped out, not the whole system like the true acid test Darwinism was supposed to demonstrate. Furthermore, the redevelopment of the system needed intelligence and intervention with a chemical that induced the gene to express a protein to allow the lactose to enter the cell (Behe, Reply to My Critics: A Response to Reviews of Darwin's Black Box: The Biochemical Challenge to Evolution, 2001).

Besides some of the tactics naturalists try to use to debunk irreducible complexity, many critics seem not to understand its definition. Behe defines it as "a single system which is composed of several well-matched, interacting parts that contribute to the basic function, and where the removal of any one of the parts causes the system to effectively cease functioning" (Behe, Darwin's Black Box, 1996). Arguments such as air bladders in certain fish turning into lungs are a misunderstanding of the concept. Air bladders and lungs are organs, not single systems. Lungs contain numerous separate irreducibly complex systems such as cilia and blood clotting that Behe discusses in *Darwin's Black Box*.

There are many examples of arguments against Behe and other ID scientists, but the examples and the evidence provided are found wanting. A Google search of irreducible complexity will demonstrate the amount of vitriol by evolutionists. They state things such as irreducible complexity debunked or "The Flagellum Unspun" or the "collapse of irreducible complexity," but these are all just smoke and mirrors and flashy hand waving. Irreducible complexity is here to stay, and is a difficult pill to swallow for evolutionists.

Injectosome

Kenneth Miller and biophysicist Matt Baker claim that the bacterial flagellum is not irreducibly complex because another similar system has been discovered that questions irreducible complexity. They refer to a secretory system of certain bacteria to demonstrate that this system has many similar proteins to the bacterial flagellum so it must be a precursor to it and consequently this system refutes irreducible complexity. But is that really the case? Just because there are similar proteins in a system homologous to proteins in the flagellum does nothing to automatically refute another system's functioning. Dr. Baker states, "Luckily, individual components of the bacterial flagellar motor have indeed been found elsewhere. And they work. So the motor is 'reducible', and certainly not 'irreducibly complex'" (Baker, 2015).

There are many reasons that Dr. Baker's "discovery" does not work. First, just because similar proteins are found elsewhere does nothing to show that a separate system can function without them. Many proteins in the human have multiple functions depending on where they are. Platelet-activating factors work in the central nervous system to help migration of neurons to the cortex during development, but they also work on the immune system in adults later in life. This does nothing to reduce the complexity of their roles in either system they function in.

Second, this particular secretory system is basically a pump that transports proteins from the inside of bacteria to the outside. It can inject toxins into other organisms and looks similar to the flagellum. However, according to Casey Luskin, "the injectisome is found in a small subset of gram-negative bacteria that have a symbiotic or parasitic association with eukaryotes (bacteria are prokaryotes, and plants and animals are eukaryotes). Since eukaryotes evolved over a billion years after bacteria, this suggests that the injectosome arose *after* eukaryotes. However, flagella are found across the range of bacteria, and the need for motility and finding food precede the need for parasitism. In other words, we'd expect that the flagellum long predates the injectosome. And indeed, given the narrow distribution of injectosome-bearing bacteria and the very wide distribution of bacteria with flagella, parsimony suggests the flagellum long predates injectosome rather than the reverse." (Luskin, 2015). Furthermore, the type-three secretory system has fewer proteins than the flagellum, so just adding several random proteins does not give you a flagellum.

Another argument that states the flagellum "devolved" into the secretory protein does not work because removing several proteins from the flagellum does not create the secretory system. Miller says that the icon of intelligent design, the flagellum, has fallen. The reverse seems to be true. The icons of evolution, the tree of life and the monkey-to-man depictions are being crushed under the weight of design in nature.

Co-option of Proteins

Evolutionists claim that irreducibly complex systems can be formed through co-option, the idea that a gene can be duplicated and the copy used for a different purpose or co-opted for the new function. This idea has been tested recently with experiments attempting to convert one protein into another (Reeves, 2014). In these experiments, attempts were made to convert one protein to be able to perform the function of a similar protein. The proteins tested were similar and in the same enzymatic family. Under the idea of co-option, the understanding is that the function of one similar protein converting to another ought to be accomplished easily. However, this was not found to be the case. The researchers found that "successful function conversion would in this case require seven or more mutations." Since it is known that protein functions or qualities that require two or more harmful mutations or over six neutral (nonthreatening and nonadvantageous) mutations before an advantage is seen would not arise in the entire 4.5-billion-year history of the earth (Axe, The Limits of Complex Adaptation: An Analysis Based on a Simple Model of Structured Bacterial Poplulations, 2010).

They then examined nine related proteins to try to change their functions to similar proteins. Single mutations were made in each of the enzymes to induce evolution of function. They discovered that a duplication of the gene would pose a disadvantage initially and that it would take 1×10^{15} years to create the necessary steps to co-opt a protein function similar to the initial protein. This is 100,000 times longer than the age of the earth (Reeves, 2014). Even with scientists intervening to try to convert the function of a protein into another similar function, it appears that the likelihood is so low that it would not happen with a single protein since before time itself began.

Differential Diagnosis

Atheism

- The design we see in nature is due to natural selection, random mutation, and genetic drift.
- Life has arisen from nonlife.
- Fine-tuning came about by chance.
- Co-opting of proteins accounts for new functions.

- Irreducible complexity is refuted.

Theism

- Design is due to an intelligence.

- Life does not arise from nonlife.
- Fine-tuning suggests an intelligence.
- Proteins have not had enough time to take on innovate new functions by random change.
- Irreducible complexity is the nail in the coffin of Darwinian evolution.

The Physician's Conclusion

The overwhelming evidence in support of design in nature is staggering. Even atheists acknowledge this but say naturalism is able to explain it better than an intelligence. An intelligent agent explains the design in the universe better than any other explanation. When all the evidence is weighed, the pretest probability that there was a designer is so strong that any other possibility is insignificant.

When patients get cervical MRIs and we look at the spinal column images and see the numbers C1, C2, C3, C4, etc., we do not assume they had their cervical vertebrae numbered by chance; it was obviously the radiologists who labeled the imaging to make them more helpful to localize where we are focusing on the images. When we see DNA and the amount of information stored and processed, it is apparent that there was an intelligence that put it there. The diagnosis is clear. The cause of information comes from a source that can create information.

The Atheist's Misdiagnosis

Natural selection doesn't have a mind; it is random. No matter what a naturalist argues, natural selection acts on random mutations. Randomness does not create design or create the illusion of design. When a person perceives design, it is due to an intelligence, not randomness. Randomness does not create anything of order. Some people may admit they have a cousin who has the intellectual capacity of a cucumber, but common sense tells us there is no relation. The God of the gaps is a sophomoric attempt to distract from the weight of the evidence against evolution. The gaps in naturalistic explanations are colossal, but atheists will guarantee an answer—in the future. We are told to just wait and be patient when all the while there is no gap in the observation that reason satisfies. There is positive evidence that design and information come from an intelligent source. The evidence points toward a Designer. The Designer does not fill a gap. Naturalism is filled with so many holes that any strain of speculative notion seems to fit as long as it does not imply God.

Cohort Study

Just as in medicine, many causes are neither sufficient nor necessary to result in an outcome by themselves. Genetic mutations are rarely sufficient or necessary to independently cause disease. Something necessary and sufficient needs to be the initial cause. Natural selection is neither sufficient nor necessary to give us something from nothing let alone the complexity and order we observe.

Something can come from nothing but only by a sufficient and necessary cause. Most people agree that the universe appears designed; it was designed or it just happens to appear that way. Since outcome 1 is what we observe, cohort 1 seems to offer the best explanation of that outcome. We observe complexity and order, and it is understood that the universe was fine-tuned for our existence; we are here and able to observe, discover, and interact with the universe.

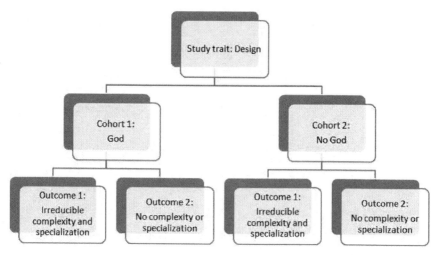

Figure 7: Cohort study evaluating the association between the
observed complexity and specialization with or without God

Cohort 1 could also result in outcome 2, but that is not what we
observe; cohort 2 is not associated with outcome 1. The observations of
irreducibly complex biological structures with cellular micromachinery, a
designer, cohort 1, is the most likely association. Not only is it associated;
it is necessary and sufficient as a cause. Information comes only from
intelligence, and that is undeniable. Information does not come from
nonintelligence let alone nothing.

CHAPTER 9

The Architect of the Cortex

For it was You who created my inward parts; You knit me together in my mother's womb.

—Psalm 139:13

This chapter is quite technical in regard to biological jargon and terminology, but the importance of biological fine-tuning cannot be understated, and the example covered underscores this necessity. We will begin by discussing a medical disorder that occurs when the process of brain development is impaired and examine the processes and biological machinery involved in building the brain architecture. The fine-tuning of the cosmos is quite exceptional, and the fine-tuning of biological mechanisms is no different.

Smooth Brain

The human cortex is highly organized. It consists of six layers organized based on function. Neuronal migration during brain development is a tightly controlled process involving countless proteins and moving pieces with several regulatory mechanisms. This is a fascinating process to say the least.

During the cortex's development, neurons move from a particular region of the developing brain and travel along a particular pathway to their designated final locations in the specific layer of the cortex. At the end of the migration, the neurons are all ordered into patterns to shape the cortex. The brain cortex is crucially designed in a certain pattern; any disruption in the process results in major biological problems. There is a spectrum of clinical disorders termed malformations of cortical development that result in disorganization of the cortex. This occurs from certain mutations in proteins involved in the process of cortical architecture development. So far, there are over a hundred genes associated with the several types of cortical migration disorders (Guerrini, 2014).

Lissencephaly is a term that was derived from ancient Greek and means smooth (*lissos*) brain (*enkephalos*); it is one disorder along the spectrum of cortical migration problems. We will pay special attention to this disorder and the underlying mechanism of why this is unique. The exact prevalence of lissencephaly is not known but is estimated to range from eleven to forty cases per million births. The clinical presentation and course of the spectrum of cortical migration disorders varies widely and depends on the amount and regions of cortex involved. Due to the impairment in neuronal movement into the cortex, the architecture is in disarray resulting in increased cortical thickness (12–20 mm compared to normal cortex, which is 3–4 mm) with only four layers instead of six. From a macroscopic view, the brain appears smooth in the affected regions (Fry, 2014).

The brain surface normally has wrinkles from the formation of gyri, but in lissencephaly, the gyri are thickened and the brain loses its wrinkly appearance. These brain defects can cause developmental delay, severe motor disability, and intellectual disability that are often serious and result in seizures and mortality often before age ten (Guerrini, 2014). Lissencephaly is associated with deletion mutations in three genes—the LIS1 gene on chromosome 17 (17p13.3) along with mutations in the genes DCX and TUBA1A (Fry, 2014). Each of these consequently lead to slowed or arrested migration of neurons during development and causes a thickened cortex with loss of folding (smooth brain).

Introduction to an Amazing Protein

The Lis1 gene encodes a highly conserved protein platelet activating factor acetylhydrolase alpha subunit 1b. About 65 percent of the mutations that cause classical lissencephaly have either whole or partial deletions in one of the LIS1 genes. We have two copies of each gene since we have twenty-three pairs of chromosomes (Fry, 2014). Absence of this gene is lethal in humans (de Rouvroit, 2001). LIS1 is a protein that is so critical in the development of the brain that it plays multiple roles. Between five and twenty-two weeks into gestation, neuroepithelial stem cells are present in the deep region of what will become the brain. Lis1 assists these cells in division into future neurons that will migrate to the cortex as well as into cells that can be thought of as tree trunks that allow for the movement of other cells up them into the cortex. The brain begins forming into the different layers that will eventually result in the cortical layers and the deep, white-matter layers at this time.

Lis1 makes up part of a three-part protein complex called the platelet activating factor acetylhydrolase (PAFAH); it typically acts to break down an inflammatory chemical in the body known as platelet activating factor (PAF). There are four known types of PAFAH in humans that are in different regions in the body. Lis1 functions in the developing brain and binds to the alpha and gamma subunits to form PAFAH (Adachi, 1995).

Why Is the Amount of This Protein so Crucial?

Most important to remember is that the amount of Lis1 is crucial to the normal development of the brain and the cortical structure. The developing brain is very sensitive to the quantity of Lis1 available to proceed with ongoing new cell generation and proper localization of the neurons (Reiner, 2013). This amazing protein is involved in multiple interactions, and the level of the protein available is critical.

The protein's initial role was thought to simply be involved with the formation of PAFAH with the alpha and gamma subunit. But we also know that when this protein binds to another protein (Ndel1) to regulate dynein movement, it does not form the trimeric structure of PAH but has a different function (Reiner, 2013). This separate role is crucial to protein transport in neurons. Of note, dynein is a molecular motor protein, and Lis1 interacts with its regulators to control its movement and transportation of cargo from the cell body down the axon to the end of the cell.

The known functions of Lis1 are (Reiner, 2013)

1. migration of neurons in cortical development
2. precise mitotic spindle orientation
   a. proliferation of neural progenitor cells
   b. kinetic nucleus positioning
3. interaction with cytoplasmic dynein for transportation

How can a single protein have so many critical roles? How can an organism's survival be so dependent on a protein that even if the organism has only 50 percent of normal amount of the protein it will not survive? If evolution explains the multiple roles of a single protein, why was it advantageous for the organism to depend so much on this protein to perform all these crucial jobs rather than the theoretical precursor protein keeping its job? We will investigate these questions by looking closer at the process of human brain cortex development.

Neuronal Migration

This protein is critical for neurons to travel from the deep region of the brain along the correct radial cells into their specific region in the cortex, for normal neuronal cell structure and for proteins (dynein) to be able to travel pathways inside of nerve cells (Yingling, 2008). Lis1 regulates dynein activity through its interaction with another protein called Ndel, which seems to connect to dynein and allows Lis1 to subsequently attach to dynein (Reiner, 2013). Without Lis1, the dynein may not be able to stay attached to the microtubule during cell division, and Lis1 allows dynein to transport high-load organelles (cell machinery) and cell vesicles (Reiner, 2013). The amount of Lis1 available seems to regulate neuronal migration and is essential for the correct pre-mitotic (mitosis is cell division) location of the nucleus (Ohtaka-Maruyama, 2015). So Lis1 acts as a guide for the neurons to be able to move from the deep portion of the developing brain outward to where they will end up in the cortex. It also helps big proteins in the nerve cell transport important things such as vesicles filled with neurotransmitters and other chemicals from the cell body to the end of the nerve. The idea of cell division can be abstract, but Lis1 helps stabilize the nucleus and keeps it in the correct location before the early nerve divides.

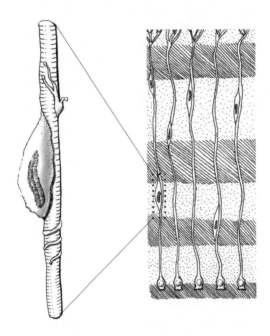

To better understand the significance of this protein, think of a pitcher in baseball. The pitcher has many roles and is the most crucial player in the game. Without the pitcher, there is no game. The pitcher has tremendous control over the organization of the game. The ability to manage several situations at a time in high-pressure situations is the hallmark of a great pitcher. The pitcher basically helps the rest of the team carry the game. Based on pitching sequence and expertise, the pitcher can make or break the team's chance of victory.

Mitotic Spindle Orientation

Cells normally divide and replicate into similar cells at an astounding rate during early development in the embryonic stages. Lis1 is essential in orienting the structure inside the replicating neuron stem cells before migration occurs. This is necessary for these stem cells to replicate appropriately into a vertically oriented plane that results in symmetric division with one proliferative daughter cell and one glial or neural cell (Yingling, 2008).

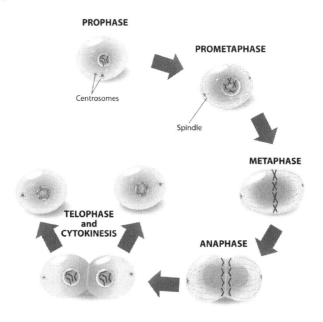

These early neural progenitor cells are deep in the brain and able to divide into two cells. One cell will be a neural progenitor cell and the other will be a neuron or a supporting cell in the brain. The neural progenitor cell is like a stem cell, but it has already started on its path to become a neuron. The supporting cell will become a cell with a different function and structure (microglial cell, astrocyte, or oligodendrocyte).

NEURONS AND NEUROGLIAL CELLS

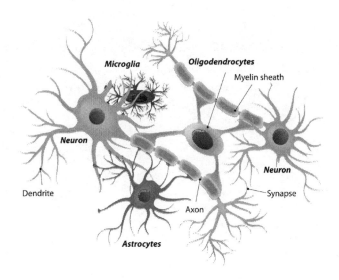

When there is not enough Lis1, the inside structure of the initial replicating neural stem cell does not align perfectly in the vertical plain, and the degree of horizontal orientation is proportional to the amount of Lis1 loss resulting in a severe and catastrophic disruption in the cortex formation (Yingling, 2008). The orientation of the neural stem cell must be precisely controlled during the symmetric dividing process. This all takes place in a short time, and if the orientation is off by a fraction, it will profoundly impair the replication of stem cells and result in a "catastrophic phenotype" (Yingling, 2008). Consequently, this results in a change of the overall fate of these neural stem cells and reduces the overall number of neurons that can migrate to the cortex.

But having more of the protein is not good either. Overexpression of Lis1 leads to the disorientation of the spindle orientation as well (de Rouvroit, 2001). This process is so important that it takes place prior to any migration of neurons or other brain-supporting cells.

Microtubule Extension and Capture in the Cortex

Another critical role Lis1 plays is with the ability of the neuron to localize properly in the correct region of the cortex. The intracellular architecture of the neural cells causes an extension of the neuron vertically toward the cortex. A formation made up of proteins called microtubules extends the cell up and out of the deep portion to reach into what will become the cortex. A moving intracellular protein called dynein travels with the help of Lis1 and helps establish the appropriate arrival region in the cortex. Without Lis1, the microtubules are shorter and do not all extend fully into the cortex. Without this protein, the microtubules are also not able to capture and hold onto the appropriate layer in the cortex (Yingling, 2008). If the cell extension is not able to grab its final position in the developing cortex, then abnormal cortical development occurs. Clinically, the amount of abnormality will depend on the amount of disruption of Lis1.

Dendrite Extension

This protein plays a role in the ability of neurons to form appropriate dendrites and the transport of proteins through the cell from one end to another (de Rouvroit, 2001). Dendrites are the arms and legs of the nerve. The dendrite is what connects to another nerve, gland, or muscle to form a synapse and communicate. Without proper Lis1, the dendrite will be dysfunctional and result in fewer synapses or poor-quality synapses.

The only explanations for the multiple critical roles of Lis1 are

1. The protein has evolved slowly from precursor proteins and subsequently taken over the roles of the other proteins due to loss of a different protein or as an advantageous takeover of another protein role.
2. The protein has gained all of the functions one by one.
3. The protein was designed to have these roles in humans.

Let's look at each of the potential options. Does the concept of co-opting account for the roles of Lis1? Since we know having too much of the protein causes the orientation of the spindle to result in abnormal cortical development, there couldn't have been a time that Lis1 was not present. Each of its roles is critical. Even a slight amount of disorientation causes catastrophic phenotypical changes.

The precursor stage prior to Lis1 having all its roles would not have survived or would not have had any advantageous qualities that natural selection would have chosen. Co-opting would cause the addition of Lis1, and we know that causes problems. So co-opting is not advantageous.

And if Lis1 was initially performing only one role, why did it need to assume the roles of other proteins? What is the advantage in such a critically precise process to depend so much on a single protein? Is there any evidence that the proteins that it superseded are still present and involved but with different roles? Without Lis1, the cortex does not form. With only 50 percent as much Lis1, the cortex is devastatingly disorganized, and with too much Lis1, the mitotic spindle orientation for neuronal cell division is dysfunctional and the cortex is impaired. There is no advantageous antecedent stage that natural selection would have chosen prior to the current Lis1 status we know now.

Could Lis1 Have Gained Each of These Functions One by One?

Either Lis1 was duplicated or it took over the function of a different protein. But the same problem occurs with co-opting. If it starts taking on a different role, there is less Lis1 available for its normal role, and that results in disorientation. The amount of the protein is crucial to normal neuronal migration. It seems to be biologically fine-tuned to a certain degree. The functional innovation of proteins would be brought about by small, successive mutations in the gene that codes for the protein. Can natural selection account for this protein gaining the new roles it has? As we have seen, most mutations are deleterious and lead to loss of function. Large-scale innovations are the cases where a protein will develop a new structure and new folding area.

Small-scale innovation are changes in DNA that result in structural adjustments of the existing assembly resulting in new function (Gauger, 2011). But we know that it appears natural selection does not allow for the appropriate new folding of proteins to gain new functions (Axe, The Case Against a Darwinian Origin of Protein Folds, 2010). Furthermore, Lis1 is critically required for each of the steps it is involved in. Why would it have been an advantage to require this protein located at one region on chromosome 17 rather than have two proteins performing the separate roles? Natural selection does not answer that question satisfactorily.

Natural selection keeps adaptable mutations, not those that lead to disadvantage. It would be more advantageous to keep the prior protein performing its own function rather than have a different protein take over the role because if there is a mutation, the survival of the organism is not as affected.

Even if we were to suppose it did take over the role of a different but similar protein, is that possible? It doesn't seem so based on the research. The small-scale innovation of a protein developing a new function that was previously held by a similar protein is very "rare becoming probable only on a time-scale much longer than the age of the earth" (Gauger, 2011). This study challenges "the conventional practice of inferring from similarity alone that transitions to new functions occurred by Darwinian evolution" (Gauger, 2011).

Differential Diagnosis

Atheism	Theism
• Humans evolved from matter.	• God created human beings and can guide any process, even natural selection and mutations if He so desires.
• Proteins can and do change structure and function causing the complexity and diversity of life.	• Proteins can change structure and function with genetic mutations, but most mutations lead to loss of function and damaged structure.
• Lis1 has multiple roles it took over from other proteins.	• Lis1 demonstrates the vital role of a single protein with multiple roles that natural selection cannot account for.

The Physician's Conclusion

Cortical architecture is not a bunch of cells layered according to color and taste. It is a highly organized structure with delicately placed cells that have gone through the precision of cell division in a perfect vertical plane of alignment. With such precision and organization, we get the cerebral cortex. It seems that it has been knitted together and managed by an architect who chooses the proper tools and pieces required. When a complicated process is so dependent on one of its components that without it, the process does not occur or it is severely disrupted, we consider it a vital element. When a process is dependent on the same component for multiple steps in the means of completion, it becomes more than vital; it becomes necessary.

Without this component, there is no product at all. The best explanation for the roles of Lis1 is that it was meant for the purposes it executes. Without it, there is no viable organism. With too little or too much, there is a nonreproducible outcome. The diagnostic conclusion is that Lis1 was designed with specific jobs to do.

The Atheist's Misdiagnosis

Natural selection does not explain the organized nature of the cerebral cortex or explain how a single protein can take on so many different roles since without it, the process doesn't even occur. Evolution cannot explain the architectural design of the neocortex. The six layers appear to have been arranged, but evolution does not give sufficient reason why these things appear to have been designed. For all of the children with genetic mutations and cortical migration defects, the offer of hope from evolution is none. The naturalist will say that there is no reason for the random mutation and that it was not an advantageous mutation. But we know from the author of Romans 8:28–29,

> We know that all things work together for the good of those who love God: those who are called according to His purpose. For those He foreknew He also predestined to be conformed to the image of His Son, so that He would be the firstborn among many brothers.

It may not be true that everything happens for a reason, but God can orchestrate anything to work for the glorification and justification of those who eagerly wait for what they do not see. The atheist misses again and uses his limited perspective of the box and is bound only by what he can see.

Cohort Study

The order and design of the cerebral cortex is dependent on many factors. With biochemical research and knowledge of lissencephaly and other cortical disorders, the dynamic and finely tuned processes of neuronal cell development and migration come to life. Outcome 1 in this cohort evaluation is so dependent on the perfect amount of Lis1. If Lis1 or another protein is modified slightly in structure or function, we get outcome 2. The point is that the cortex is not dependent on a single protein with a single function; rather, the cortex structure and proper function for normal cognition and mobility are dependent on many proteins and Lis1 has more than one critical role. Cohort 2 with evolutionary mechanisms as the main explanation does not offer a reasonable way to get outcome 1. Cohort 2 doesn't offer a way to get outcome 2.

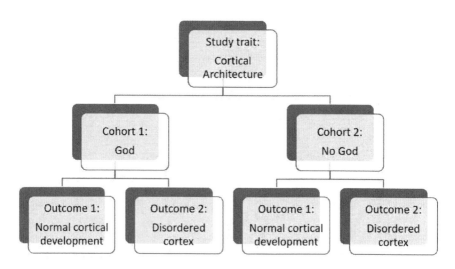

Figure 8: Cohort design for evaluating the appearance and structure of the human cerebral cortex

Based on natural selection, Lis1 would never exist and would not have more than one life-sustaining role. Cortical migration cannot be explained by unguided genetic mutations acted upon by a process such as natural selection. Both outcomes 1 and 2 are best associated with cohort 1. We observe both outcomes 1 and 2. They cannot be observed in cohort 2.

CHAPTER 10

You Are Not Your Brain

Love the Lord your God with all your heart, with all your
soul, with all your strength, and with all your mind.

—Luke 10:27

Inside Out

My family and I have enjoyed the 2015 Disney/Pixar animated film *Inside
Out* that basically takes place inside a young girl's brain. As a neurologist,
I was fascinated by the plot. A Pixar animated film about the brain?
Awesome!

The theme is educational for children in that it demonstrates the
importance of emotions and that sadness is a critical element in adequate
mental maturation. The visual animated workings inside the brain were
great. Though the movie was simplified, its handling of long-term memory
and core memory elements were entertaining.

The way the core memories of the young girl, Riley, are intricately
tied to her emotional experiences has quite a bit of truth. The disposal of
outgrown and useless memories in the memory dump has some component
of fact as well. Most of all, the way that Riley's physical brain is managed
by all the little creatures is analogous to our physical brains being run or
managed by something other than themselves.

The idea that something other than the brain controls what it does seems to assume a nonphysical factor that gives the orders. In the movie, that nonphysical factor is depicted mainly by the four emotions—fear, sadness, anger, and joy. In real life, the nonphysical factor is the mind. The mind tells the brain what to do, and the brain relays and interprets information for the mind. Clearly in the movie, Riley was for the most part able to maintain control over her life and behaviors, but the emotions were able to manipulate or guide many of the choices she made.

Riley went through the struggles of life and discovered joy in the midst of sadness. The ultimate transformation of character comes through the struggles in life. It was a great ending! The family did not choose the easy thing for their daughter by just moving back to Minnesota, where her old friends were. Though that would have made her temporarily happy, the family needed to work through the difficulties of the move to San Francisco. The movie depicted the new memories as a mixture of the different emotions; there became a combination of emotional memories such as joy, sadness, fear, and anger. Just as in reality, as Riley ages, maybe the emotions won't have as much control over her choices or actions. We look forward to a sequel!

What Is the Mind?

In the neurology clinic, patients often say, "My brain doesn't do what I want" or "I can't get my brain to remember things." If the brain is who we are, why do we refer to it as just another body part? These statements wouldn't sound strange if the patients were referring to their legs or their hearts—"I can't get my leg to do what I want" or "My heart won't stop beating so fast." These make complete sense in that we do not regard our hearts or legs as being able to form thoughts or make decisions. Why do we give that power to our brains? What was Jesus referring to in Luke 10 when He instructed us to love the Lord with all our mind?

Eleven Greek words in the New Testament refer to the mind. The Greek word used for mind in Luke 10 is *dianoia*—character, intention, or will. Another Greek word for mind specifically in Romans 12:2 and 1 Corinthians 2:16 is *nous*—the intellect and understanding (Strong, 2007). So Jesus was commanding us to love God with our hearts, physical strength, souls, and our character, intent, and will. Romans 12 instructs us to be "transformed by the renewing of our minds," nous, which refers to our intellectual mind so we can discern what is good and pleasing to God. We are instructed to use our minds for God's glory and not to be idle in our thoughts.

The mind is nonphysical. The ability to have a thought about a physical object (a new pickup truck I'm envious of!) cannot be attributed to a physical entity. Our thoughts are private and cannot be known to the public without our expressing them through speech or action. A thought cannot be explained physically but only through personal explanation, so it must not be material.

The Brain Cannot Explain the Mind

Crudely speaking, the brain comprises a clump of different cells. The heart is also made up of a clump of different cells. What makes them function so differently? Brain cells use a mechanism of sending signals based on voltage differences between the inside and outside of the cell. When a nerve cell is activated, sodium and potassium passively and actively move in and out of the cell creating a voltage or charge difference between the outside and inside of the cell. This propagates along the nerve axon to the appropriate synapse and talks to the next cell by causing activation or inhibition. This process is called depolarization of the cell. Cardiac cells use depolarization and voltage differences to propagate along each other to continue contracting the cardiac muscle so the heart can beat appropriately.

The physiology is similar. The biochemistry of the brain is not what forms our minds, personalities, preferences, or desires. The biochemistry of my brain is not why I love chocolate. There is no neurological biochemical pathway for chocolate lovers. There is no neuroanatomic correlate for why I love baseball or why I love my family. The brain does not give us self-awareness. We do not lose our humanness when the brain does not work. If we did lose our human value when our brain shuts off, anyone in a coma would not truly be considered human. The brain does not explain the mind.

The Brain Is Physical—The Mind Is Not

When our brains are sick or injured, our bodies do not work as well. This is no surprise; it doesn't take neuroscience to tell us that. If we lose an arm, it doesn't work anymore. The brain is made up of cells with connections. The heart is made up of cells with connections. According to Darwinian evolution, the human brain has gained the capability of self-awareness and self-consciousness other animals do not possess. At which point does this occur? Picture this with me briefly as we run through this scenario. Imagine millions of years ago a group of apes or simians doing their ape things such as beating their chests and checking each other for bugs. A new member is born in their community with a new mutation that causes one extra connection in the brain that all of a sudden allows it self-awareness. As the new member with self-consciousness grows and develops, she recognizes her abilities and is able to compare herself to her friends. She is not like the other members because she can focus on herself unlike her friends. This ability to self-focus and retain a sense of "Who or what am I" is not understood by the other members, so she feels different and isolated from them. How would this be advantageous for this member of the community to develop the sense of self-awareness? At what point does that happen from a materialistic view?

It doesn't seem that evolution explains this development. Scientific determinism is the idea that there is a naturalistic explanation for everything. This includes our ability to form thoughts and execute certain behaviors. Based on scientific determinism, our behaviors are just neurons firing and resulting in actions. Our ability to make the right decisions is an evolutionary power, and if we choose poorly, that's just one of the disadvantages of the maladaptive traits we have inherited or acquired.

According to this idea, all the suffering and poor decisions in the world can be explained by brains misfiring and resulting in poor actions rather than free will of people using their minds. But that does not make sense because plenty of people take advantage of being good liars and making bad decisions. So what defines a bad decision? Only one that seems to disagree with a naturalist. They do not have a good explanation for the existence of the mind, but through the appeal to promissory materialism, we are supposed to just trust that science will have the answer sometime in the future.

Neuroscientist Mario Beauregard stated that materialism was limited as a philosophical supposition in this regard "in which problems with the assumptions of the system are simply deferred to future science; they do no result in a critical examination of the system itself" (Beauregard, 2007). Dr. Beauregard refers to promissory materialism this way: "If we adopt it, we are accepting a promissory note on the future of materialism" (Beauregard, 2007). Nobel Prize laureate and neuroscientist John Eccles stated,

> We regard promissory materialism as superstition without a rational foundation. The more we discover about the brain, the more clearly do we distinguish between the brain events and mental phenomena, and the more wonderful do both the brain events and the mental phenomena become. (Eccles, 1984)

Two Minds?

The brain is definitely a complex organ, but just because there are many connections does not account for its presence. The kidney is a complex organ with multiple connecting cells and structures, but its number or type of connections does not create consciousness or self-awareness. There is not a magic number of nerve synapses that once you reach it, voilà, you have self-awareness. The heart does not develop self-awareness of its existence based on just the chemical communication and connections with other cells. If the chemical connections and the number of synapses were what created the mind, why don't we develop more minds? Why is it best to have just one mind?

In abnormal psychology, there are disorders of multiple personalities or split personalities, but this isn't because of more connections or better neurotransmission. Why does natural selection think that for each body only one mind is best?

Why Trust Chemicals?

If naturalism were true, our thoughts are nothing but cause and effect. We shouldn't really have to think at all. Our hearts automatically beat without our conscious awareness, so shouldn't our brains just decide matters for us as well? Isn't that the implication of a completely physical process? But that is not what we experience. As C. S. Lewis has pointed out, why would we trust our own conclusions and interpretations about anything if they were just atoms and chemicals? What makes one person's cause and effect of physical neurotransmitters any better than someone else's? What makes a person believe his or her neurochemicals? It is basically just an organized neurochemical stew of action and reaction? Why should I believe anyone else's cerebral static was right and mine was wrong? Why try to convince anyone if you believe that?

The Ability to Argue

Why would I trust anyone else's brain chemicals over mine? Who is to say his or her brain is signaling better than mine? Atheists want us to believe they must have the correct connections and brain chemicals, but how do they know that, and why should we believe them?

The ability to argue one's case is one of the best and most powerful arguments for the existence of God. We can debate and argue God's existence; that seems to infer an intelligibility beyond ourselves. The inference is there whether or not we are aware of it. For example, atheists write books arguing that there is no God and that we are all products of nonliving material. Why would I believe that over any other book? Why should I believe the idea that our minds are made up of just chemicals? Isn't that idea just a random assortment of chemicals that caused the thought to be written on paper? This is irrational and similar to writing a book on why it is important not to write books.

If the mind is a random-chance physical object, all its results are random effects without rational intelligibility. But we know that is not the case. We know that the products of the mind are rational and purposeful. An atheist wants everyone to believe what they write in their books, but what does it matter if the mind is just a bunch of cells and chemicals and static?

Will Computers Have Souls Some Day?

With the explosive advent of the technological revolution and the advance of computer innovation, there has been increasing discomfort with the thought of artificial intelligence. The movies *AI* and *I, Robot* portray machines that develop emotions and self-awareness. But is that possible? Can a computer or a machine actually learn to appreciate beauty, sadness, fear, or brotherly love? Where do these feelings come from? Can we chalk them up to biochemical signals responding to environmental stimuli? Or are they more likely to be properties of a nonphysical constituent such as a mind? Do neurotransmitters such as dopamine or GABA explain emotions?

From functional brain imaging, we know that strong emotions from visual stimuli change the functioning in certain parts of the brain, but that could be the brain responding to the emotions rather than causing the emotions. Computers may appear that they are responding when they are really just running on programs that follow instructions.

Views of Consciousness

There are a few different ideas of what human consciousness is. One is called property dualism or nonreductive physicalism. This view believes that consciousness and thought are caused completely by physical properties and are material. This view does not believe in the soul. According to property dualism, if we could form a computer with the same connections as the brain, it could potentially develop consciousness (Hoskins, 2016).

The other view is substance dualism, which states there is a body and there is a soul. According to substance dualism, the soul can exist apart from the body. Most people who hold this view believe the body and the soul must be descended from another human being and so nonhuman objects cannot be granted a soul (Hoskins, 2016). This is important because of the value of the soul and the doctrine of God's creation of man and woman. With a nonreductive physicalist view, we would annihilate the soul and with it our value as eternally created beings.

Mind Disorder

Because we possess a mind, a greater mind seems to be inferred. This is because a mind cannot come from nonmind and certainly not from nonlife. Intelligence alone does not explain the mind or consciousness. As we have seen, a computer can be intelligent, but it cannot be conscious. In medicine, we witness the mind doing extraordinary things. A disorder that has been well explained for centuries, conversion disorder, is a disorder of the mind over the body. The term conversion means that a stressful emotion is "converted" into a physical response. For example, psychogenic seizures are a form of conversion disorder (the term *conversion disorder* was coined by Sigmund Freud). People with these forms of seizures do not have epilepsy, but they suffer from uncontrollable convulsions due to the mind controlling the body. This differs from a brain disorder such as epilepsy. In epilepsy, there are abnormal areas of the brain that are firing haphazardly causing spread of firing neurons and resulting in clinical seizures. This can be seen on electroencephalography (EEG) with certain abnormal brain wave activity.

But with psychogenic seizures, the EEG is normal even during an episode. This is basically diagnostic of psychogenic seizures/convulsions. In this disorder, the mind has an amazing capacity to take over control of the body and the brain and cause a potentially dangerous and debilitating problem. Antiseizure medications do not work for these seizures because they are not epileptic in nature. The patients unfortunately are not able to control their seizures without mental health management. They are not faking their seizures, but the seizures are not explained by a brain problem or any other physiologic (natural) problem. These are beyond a physical cause because they are disorders of the mind.

Another example of conversion disorder is psychogenic blindness. Some people can go blind due to a severely traumatic event. However, ophthalmologic examination and testing is normal. The pupils dilate, the optic nerve picks up light and motion, and brain imaging and testing is normal. Nonetheless, the person literally cannot see though there is nothing physically wrong with his or her eyes, optic nerves, or brain. Again, the mind has converted an emotional response into a physiological response, blindness.

The Placebo Effect

In medicine, the placebo effect is real. If someone takes something that could possibly help, they can get a benefit regardless of whether it was due to the medication's action, or whether the person just perceived a benefit, or if the body truly responded positively because of the effect of the mind. This is a mystery in medicine and science. The physical and material world cannot explain the placebo effect. Sometimes, even showing up at the doctor's office can start making someone feel better as they may consider that the beginning to the healing process.

There is something about the body's response to the mind. Similar to conversion disorders that we have discussed, the body can respond to the mind's process of what is taking place. The placebo effect can be powerful enough to help reduce pain and other physical dysfunctions. This is basically a nonmaterial, nonphysical process that results in improvement in physical problems. In randomized, double-blinded clinical studies of multiple sclerosis where no patient or doctor knows who is getting a placebo or actual medication, the placebo study group and the actual medication study group both show a reduction in annual relapse rates. Yet no one knows who is getting a placebo or actual medication. If those being studied don't know they are getting real medication versus a placebo such as a saline solution, why would they have less inflammation causing a brain or spinal cord flare-up? How can anything physical explain the actual physical change in the immune system? Something nonphysical reduces the activity of the immune system in the placebo group, whereas the actual medication being studied decreases the activity of the immune system in the study group.

Differential Diagnosis

Atheism

The mind does not exist as a nonphysical entity.
Scientific determinism explains human's actions and illusion of free will.
Computers are able to gain a level consciousness.

Theism

The mind is nonphysical and thoughts are not measurable, objective entities.
Free will exists and is nonphysical.
Human beings are made in the image of God, and consciousness has intrinsic value and worth.

The Physician's Conclusion

People make their own decisions, which have consequences. Most decisions we make do not tend to be advantageous to us, and we end up paying for them later. Things that are difficult at the time often pay off bigger dividends later in life. If naturalism were true, we would be better at delaying gratification because of its advantages in survival. However, the opposite is true; we seem to be getting worse at delayed gratification. Furthermore, every doctor knows that patients' brains do not do what they want them to do. Where does that come from? What do we mean when we say, "I want my brain to work better"? If you are your brain, whom are you referring to?

It appears to be common sense that we all have knowledge and are more than just our brains. Biologists and anatomists should easily realize that the brain is another organ made up of connecting cells. The connections do not explain thoughts and intangibles. We all know that a mind cannot come from dirt and time; that doesn't happen. That's not how things work. It is highly speculative and imaginary to suggest that a thinking, conscious, relational mind pops into being from lifeless stuff. It is not science to suggest that is the best explanation of the mind. Science does not point to neurons causing us to be able to make decisions based on our desires. Knowledge never seems to guarantee the result since we are well aware of the negative consequences yet tend to choose poorly much of the time. If it were up to our brains alone to "decide," it seems we wouldn't have to think about anything. Just like the heart beating, the brain should be automatically making our decisions for us.

The Atheist's Misdiagnosis

This is the worst case of misdiagnosis I have ever come across. All physicians misdiagnosis things now and then, but when it is obvious and staring at us in the face, there's no excuse.

To atheists, the mind is hard to dismiss as a physical entity. The fact that atheists write books to persuade us that our minds are just our brains is evidence the mind exists. Why bother writing a book just to say our minds are just chemical processes? What does it matter if my brain chemicals result in me not agreeing with your book? Why try to change my brain chemicals? How did your brain chemicals and connections make you write that book that explains why your mind is just chemicals? Why on earth should I trust your brain more than anyone else's?

Cohort Study

If reality is exposed to the nonexistence of God, there is no mind. A mind cannot come from nothing. We observe outcome 1. But naturalists say we observe outcome 2. If that is true, why try to make my cerebral static like yours? What does it matter if the brain chemicals result in the agreement that outcome 2 is correct? It would be similar to trying to change my heart rate to be like theirs just because it beats a little faster or trying to get my blood pressure into the agreeable range.

But consciousness and thoughts are nonobjective, nonphysical things and the mind is separate from the physical brain. The will to act or behave is not chemical. The mind tells the brain to send the chemical to coordinate the act or behavior. Outcome 1 cannot occur in the setting of cohort 2 as a mind cannot result from a nonmind. Consciousness cannot emerge from the lifeless. Outcome 1 is what is observed and is best explained as a causal association with cohort 1.

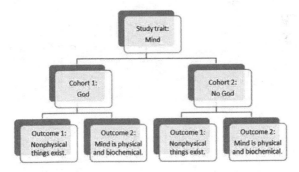

Figure 9. Cohort study evaluating the existence of nonphysical properties such as the mind

CHAPTER 11

Order and Reliability

Your faithfulness is for all generations; You established the
earth, and it stands firm.

—Psalm 119:90

God Is Reliable

If God exists, He must be reliable. How else could we be expected to trust
anything? If God is not faithful and reliable, why would we be expected to
rely on His disclosure to us in His general revelation of nature or His special
revelation of scripture? But we know from scripture we can trust Him to
do what He says. He is the most reliable Being that could exist. So if that is
the case, we can trust His general revelation of His creation is also reliable.

The Study of Nature Must Be Reliable

If we are expected to learn about the nature of God through His general
revelation of His creation, it should be reliable enough for us to study it
and use it to expect certain results. For example, in the fine-tuning of the
universe, certain constants have been discovered. By definition, these values
were set as constants so we can use them and rely on them to discover more.
Without this reliability, we would be in a heap of trouble. We wouldn't be

able to run any scientific experiments. Ultimately, there would be nothing to expect as a result of the experiment because any result could be expected. We would not be able to test a hypothesis to see if it is true because without the reliability of nature, we couldn't expect anything specific. We could get any set of results and it would be impossible to reliably test the hypothesis.

By definition, God is faithful and has set the attributes of nature in line with His divine attributes so we can study it and learn about Him. This raises the question as to why the universe looks so old. Either it is actually 15 billion years old or it just looks that way. But why would a faithful God just make the universe look old to us? He sure could do that if He wanted to, but scripture teaches us that He is faithful and He does not trick us. He said that His existence is evident to us in His creation. He gives us creation to steward and learn from. He gave us the natural constants to study and learn about Him, not for us to be confused about. Because of the order and reliability of nature, we can be confident God is also reliable. The second law of thermodynamics demonstrates the natural progression toward disorder and equilibrium and that it takes work to maintain order.

Where Does Reliability Come From?

When we think about what is reliable, we are referring to the expectation that something will be repeatable. For example, we expect the sun to rise in the east every twenty-four hours. We expect Old Faithful to erupt every ninety or so minutes. We expect certain aspects of nature to be reliable and repeatable in order to test them, and we attribute reliability to human beings as well. Reliability requires order. There must be a structure to things for us to expect a certain outcome. Order can come only from an intelligent source, not from nothing or chance. If things were left to chance, we would not see order but rather complete disorder.

Experiments Need Order

The scientific method requires order for repeatability. To replicate an experiment and build the case for a hypothesis or theory, we need to be able to reproduce the results. If we cannot reproduce the results of a study, we cannot verify whether the results are true. We would be able to design studies for our hypotheses and come up with any results we please because we know that no one else would be able to replicate them. Good research is repeatable. Due to the reliability of nature, we can trust the results we get; God won't allow us to get results inconsistent with creation.

Science relies on nature's order and reliability. If I designed an experiment that required water to boil, I would expect that to occur every time during the experiment at approximately 100 degrees Celsius here on earth. The boiling point of water depends also on atmospheric pressure, but it is quite reliable as long as that is known as well. There is an expected order to it that can be relied upon to produce repeatable results. Without this, there cannot be any experiment able to be reproduced. This includes all scientific achievements throughout history including the theory of gravity and all others. The only explanation for why gravity exists in the first place is because of an intelligent mind who knew all of this beforehand. It cannot be overstated that order cannot come from disorder without intelligent effort and guidance.

Isn't Order Just an Illusion?

The argument that design and order are illusory does not work in reality. There is intrinsic knowledge we depend on for things to function properly. If we just pretended there is no order, things would fall apart. Arguing that reliability is just an illusion that we make up in our brains is speculative and imaginative; no one practices that. We all rely on things to work according to how they are "supposed" to.

The Laws of Nature

Order does not come from the laws of nature; the laws of nature are ordered. These laws do not explain why there is order; they describe the order that is present. Nature is ordered and reliable, and our mathematical descriptions demonstrate it. Science cannot answer the question as to what the purpose of order is. A naturalist would say the answer doesn't matter. But why are we able to even wonder and ask that question? If science is incapable of answering the question, we must appeal to something besides science. A bee is attracted to flowers in order to pollinate. Hydrogen is attracted to oxygen. Thank God for order.

The Physician's Conclusion

Order and reliability are qualities of the God of the Bible. They cannot come from nothing. Just like the immaterial order, life and society are ordered. There is structure to everything, and that infers design. The human body is no exception. In medicine, we train for years to learn what the normal systems are like and how they function. Without a grasp of the normal order, there is no discerning what is not normal or in disorder. Without a known standard of normal neurological physical exam, there would be no way to tell if a person's neurological exam is abnormal. There would be no need to use the neurological examination to aid in diagnosis. In fact, without the normal, there would be no abnormal.

This is similar to the argument of morality in that there is also an objective standard model on which to test every other model. We expect there to be something to make a comparison so we can make a reasonable determination if it is in line with the normal or not. Even in the most basic structures of life and nonlife there appears to be order. DNA has such a unique order that it produces language and information. Language can come only from consciousness. That is why we don't see objects producing language (though the heavens do seem to declare the glory of God!).

Every patient must be compared to the normal to determine if there is something abnormal. Where does the normal come from? It has to come from order that is clearly from a conscious mind.

The Atheist's Misdiagnosis

Naturalism has no way to explain order and reliability, but naturalists are happy to appeal to the order around us to stabilize and regulate their lives. Order in nature is critical to survival and cannot come from disorder. There is no evidence that natural selection can result in ordered designs or mechanisms. There is no evidence that with enough time, order comes about from nonorder. For the atheist, the only way to reconcile their problem of order is to deny it exists. Just like all the other evidence around us, the continual denial of its existence as an illusion continues to be the default explanation. Again, this is not satisfactory to any sincere seeker of knowledge and truth as it does not quench the thirst for the best explanation.

They will refer to the absurd notion that order is illusory and that there does not have to be an explanation for why things appear ordered. This is highly problematic and another example of the impracticality of atheism. If order is illusory, the next time an atheist wants to take medications for an illness, just let him know he can take any dose he wants at any time because it doesn't matter which order he takes them because they're just an illusion.

Cohort Study

As we have discovered, reliability and order are the way reality is and there is no explanation how this could come from nonmind and nonlife. We clearly see outcome 1 and the best association is through cohort 1. Outcome 2 is not what we see, but it is the only explanation from the materialist proponents. They have to appeal to either the nonexistence of order or as order as an illusion of the brain. But that does not explain it either since we rely on the order in nature for us to study the universe. Without repeatable and predictable components to the universe, the results of experiments could not be relied on. The impracticality and absurdity of the naturalists' explanations are suspect in regard to the claims that science can provide us satisfactory answers.

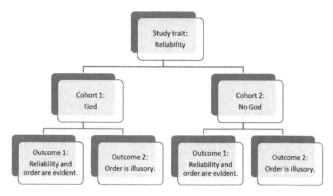

Figure 10: Cohort study evaluating the existence nonphysical properties such as the reliability and order

PART III

THE DIAGNOSIS AND CAUSE

CHAPTER 12

Diagnosis

The case for God is not based on isolated evidence but on cumulative and coherent arguments for His existence. It is time to review the observations and the evidence provided for the existence of God. We have seen that there are several arguments for and against the existence of a spaceless, timeless, immaterial, all-powerful, loving, sustaining, personal God.

Let's first use the neurological localization technique from the clinical side of things. As you may remember from earlier chapters, we neurologists take pride in our neurological examination techniques. We are usually able quite quickly to determine if symptoms are coming from the nervous system or not. When a patient presents with a neurological problem, based on the history and the exam, we can localize what and where the problem is coming from. If someone has weakness of the eyelid muscle that improves with application of ice and worsens with staring upward for one minute, we can localize that to the neuromuscular junction (the region between a nerve and a muscle). If a sixty-five-year-old man presents to the clinic with one year of progressive weakness of the forearm muscles bilaterally but only the ones that help with wrist and finger flexion, and has weakness of the quadriceps, we think about an inflammatory muscle disorder called inclusion body myositis.

A healthy teenager who has had two to three weeks of slowly ascending weakness of the legs up to the trunk and has no reflexes localizes to multiple spinal nerve roots in a disorder termed acute demyelinating inflammatory polyradiculoneuropathy (ADIP) and he needs to be treated urgently.

The localization is crucial to the course of the disorder. When we apply the evidence available to the cause of the universe and the way things are, the localization is also crucial as it shapes the way we see the world and how we respond to it.

Localizing God

As we have seen in the previous chapters, there are several explanations for all the observations we have made. But with all of the evidence, the most consistent entity that can account for all these is a transcendent being. We know from physics that the universe had a beginning. Matter, space, and time all had a beginning, but we also know from common sense and science that things don't just come into existence by themselves. So a timeless, spaceless, and immaterial being had to cause them. It localizes easily.

Next, we know that in order to fine-tune the conditions necessary for our existence and sustenance, the creator must be all-powerful, intelligent, and sustaining. Like an orchestra, the music must be sustained for it to continue. This is the same as with the continuation of existence. The creator must have been personal and not abstract. Abstract necessary entities are not creative, so that leads to a personal cause.

Finally, an all-loving cause must exist in order to share the creation with the creature. Moreover, an all-loving being must allow it the opportunity to not love it back. Love is the act of giving of self and not expecting it in return. Love is sacrificial, not self-centered. A self-centered god would have created the universe and his creatures and forced them to love him. We are not droids; we are able to deny God. All the evidence localizes away from chance and toward a spaceless, timeless, immaterial, all-powerful, loving, sustaining, personal Creator. This sounds a lot like the God of the Bible, and this is without even opening a single book of the Bible.

Localization and Coherency

Neurological localization of a disorder depends also on the coherency between the findings. If different exam findings don't fit with each other, the cause needs to be reexamined. For example, if a patient has inability to lift the right foot at the ankle (foot drop) and has double vision, we may think of something such as multiple sclerosis. If it were due to multiple sclerosis, we would suspect the eyes would not track objects together when looking different directions that improves when closing one eye. We would expect exaggerated reflexes on the effected side along with a finding called the Babinski sign (the large toe extends up when the bottom of the foot is touched). However, on exam of this patient, we see that the double vision is present in both eyes and does not change when either eye is closed. The ankle weakness demonstrates normal Achilles' reflex and no evidence of Babinski sign. From a neurological standpoint, these would seem unrelated in this patient. The most common cause of this type of double vision is something such as dry eyes. And a common cause of this type of ankle weakness is a nerve injury near the knee or a nerve root pinched in the lower back.

This sort of localizing exam is the same thing we can do with the coherency of the arguments from the different worldviews. All the arguments for the existence of God maintain this internal coherency. Atheism runs into this localization problem right off the bat between the cosmological explanation along with the teleological explanation. God is a plausible explanation for the beginning of time, space, matter, and energy, and this coheres with the fine-tuning argument of a fine-tuner. The atheist is left with the beginning of time, space, matter, and energy coming from nothing by nothing. How is this coherent with the fine-tuning we see in order for sapient life to exist? The atheist must say that chance is the best explanation. But we have seen the probability of that is virtually zero. It appears that the denial of God seems to be simpler than submitting to Him. Since the explanations of naturalism are not coherent, it takes much greater faith to believe the evidence is in the atheist's favor.

Definite Diagnosis

Let's move on and apply the 2010 McDonald MS diagnostic criteria to the evidence.

The diagnosis depends on the amount of evidence available, the specificity of the evidence, and the evaluation of other possible explanations.

If you recall from earlier in the book, a definite diagnosis of MS will require two clinical or historical events that are specific for MS and two objective findings consistent with MS. Supportive evidence such as brain and cervical MRI lesions consistent with MS is helpful as well.

1. Are there at least two clinical/historical events that are more consistent with the existence of God as the explanation?
   a. The cosmological arguments including the Thomist, Kalam, and Leibnizian arguments all make very compelling historical cases for the existence of God. With these claims and the arguments in favor of each premise, the existence of God seems more plausible than not. To answer the question of why anything exists rather than nothing is best explained by an immaterial and timeless creator.
   b. The existence of morals implies a moral lawgiver. A sense of morals does not seem to come from sociobiological conditioning alone but is objective and not explained by each person's preference. A sense of duty and value is intrinsic as a standard that humans seem to possess. The best explanation of an objective standard fits best with a God who sets the standard.
2. Are there at least two objective findings that indicate an intelligence beyond nature?
   a. The multitude of fine-tuning quantities in the universe including the precise values of the fundamental forces in addition to the uniqueness and location of our solar system and planet point to an intelligence that must have created this set of variables for life to originate, sustain, and discover the creation.
   b. The countless biological systems and machines that appear to be designed for their particular functions and are not explainable by time and chance alone. The specified complexity of biological systems and the order and design of the cerebral cortex is architecturally manufactured and requires intricate amounts of necessary proteins.

3. Are there any other supportive findings that would indicate God as the cause?
   a. The universe as an interacting whole is best explained by something that is transcendent and immaterial.
   b. The existence of the mind and consciousness demonstrates that there is more than the physical.
4. Are there any other better explanations or possible mimickers?
   a. Naturalism does not explain the origin of time or space since we know nothing comes from nothing by nothing.
   b. Moral duties and values are objective and beyond just the physical, so naturalism does not provide a good explanation.
   c. Chance cannot explain the fine-tuning of the universe, solar system, and our planet.
   d. Natural selection acting on random mutations does not explain why there are protein machines that perform specific functions that require each particular protein in order to work.
   e. Naturalism cannot explain why the universe requires all its parts in order to exist and why all the parts require the whole to exist. Without the one, the other doesn't exist. Naturalism cannot explain the universe and its parts.
   f. The mind is metaphysical and beyond scientific explanation. The best explanation of the origin and existence of the finite mind and consciousness is an infinite mind and consciousness.

Based on the cumulative examination of the evidence, it is quite clear that a definite diagnosis can be made for the cause of the universe—God. There is no more plausible explanation than that. With all the evidence presented and weighed, no physician would continue to wonder if that is the correct diagnosis. We are trained not to speculate on possibilities. As we have seen, the specificity of these criteria is very high at 93 percent, so it will accurately exclude the wrong diagnosis 93 percent of the time. That is overwhelmingly accurate in medicine. Furthermore, the positive predictive value (the strength of the test to correctly predict the outcome with few false positives) of the criteria is 94 percent. This is such strong evidence that we consider it a definite diagnosis because it easily meets all the tested criteria. When a patient meets all the criteria to that extent, there is no question in neurology as to the correct diagnosis. When we are fortunate enough to have that much evidence, it would take a lot of self-effort and self-delusion to convince that it is not the correct diagnosis. When a person fits the diagnostic criteria so fully but a different physician makes the claim that the patient most likely has some other diagnosis, we would naturally believe he or she was joking.

CHAPTER 13

Association and Causal Inference

We can examine the evidence even more using epidemiological statistics and further build the case for the weight of this evidence that points to the existence of God. As you may remember, a cohort study helps to determine if there is an association between an observation (disease, outcome) and an exposure (cohort group).

Throughout these chapters, we have designated God as the exposure in cohort 1 and atheism as no exposure in cohort 2. Disease is the way that things are, and our current observations have been designated as outcomes 1 and 2. We will determine whether the cumulative evidence we have is better explained by the exposure group or the group without the exposure. Remember, a cohort study is designed to determine whether there is an association between the exposure and the outcome, but it does not tell us whether the exposure is the cause of the disease. We will need to filter through causal inference to determine if an association is causal. But let's first look at the modified cohort study.

Cohort 1 (God)		Cohort 2 (No God)	
Outcome 1	Outcome 2	Outcome 1	Outcome 2
something from nothing by something	something from nothing by nothing	something from nothing by something	something from nothing by nothing
objective moral values and duties exist	no objective morals exist	objective moral values and duties exist	no objective morals exist
interacting components and whole	independent components and whole	interacting components and whole	independent components and whole
nonphysical properties exist	mind is physical and biochemical	nonphysical properties exist	mind is physical and biochemical

For there to be an association between disease and exposure, the proportion of diseased with exposure must outweigh the diseased without exposure. Based on this summarized table, outcome 1 is what is observed. Outcome 1 is best explained as occurring with cohort 1 in all the observational studies. There may be more arguments on both sides for the outcome, but Darwinian naturalism is limited in its ability to offer more explanations for the way we observe things to be. As we have seen, the main Darwinian arguments for everything have to do with something coming from nothing by nothing, chance, and natural selection acting on mostly random occurrences.

All the arguments for the outcome with God are unique and plausible. The arguments for outcome 1 from cohort 2 are similar and limited. The weight of the cumulative evidence is that there is an association between the observable world (outcome 1) and the exposure (God). It is less likely that there is an association between the observable world (outcome 1) and no exposure (no God). This is compelling evidence since we know that these studies compare the weight of each argument not against each other but against the likely relationship of a potential etiology. Smoking (exposure) is associated with lung cancer (disease) even though many people who get lung cancer (disease) have never smoked (no exposure), but the number of smokers who get lung cancer exceeds the number of nonsmokers who get lung cancer. The more plausible the explanation that the existence of God produces the outcomes that we see, the more likely the causal relation.

Causation

Outcome 1 is the way that reality is and is most plausibly related to cohort 1 rather than cohort 2. Since an association is made, we can determine whether the association is actually causally related or not.

1. Temporal relation: Was the cause prior to the effect?
   a. The evidence shows that the universe had to have been created by a timeless and spaceless being. We know logically that something cannot create itself since that implies that it exists prior to its existence. Based on scientific data, matter, time, space, and energy all had a beginning (cause) that was present prior to the effect.
2. Strength: The higher the probability, the more likely it is causal.
   a. The probability that the fine-tuning of the constants and other variables for the existence of life in the universe and this solar system occurred perfectly by chance is so small that it is much more likely that an intelligence set the precise values. We have seen that the numbers that the fine-tuning of the universe occurred by chance is virtually zero and demands a different explanation. Not only is chance basically ruled out, but also, the impeccably chosen numbers in relation to each other infer a Tuner.
   b. The so-called anthropic principle that we are here to observe the universe because that's the way it had to be does nothing to offer an explanation as to why it is the way it is.
3. Replication of findings: We would expect to see the same thing in other groups and populations
   a. We observe that the laws of nature are constant throughout the universe.

b. The order of the universe allows scientists to expect certain conditions and outcomes and is not explained by anything other than a designer.

c. Without the order of things (gravity), things would be absurd and unpredictable and scientific studies would not work. Unguided processes such as natural selection do not result in order.

4. Alternative explanations: Are there multiple plausible explanations?

a. Natural selection and chance cannot explain the existence of anything.

b. Natural selection can explain some of the diversity through microevolution, but that does not necessarily lead to the development of new species.

5. Cessation of exposure: If the removal of the cause decreases the effect, it is causal.

a. Since the "Death of God" movement in the twentieth century, we have witnessed the bloodiest and deadliest time in history. Without God, the world does not work. Without God, there is no universe or existence. Without God, there is no hope.

Internal Coherency

The Christian God has disclosed His existence, and the weight of the evidence is substantial. The universe has a diagnosis. Not only is the evidence important, but also, the internal coherency between explanations confirms the conclusion. The fact that a loving God created the universe and allows human free will knowing that we would cause such misery and suffering by our choices that He comes to this place as a human to experience the humiliating suffering death fulfills all of the explanations consistently. Naturalism's numerous inherent inconsistencies are profound. The idea of material transforming into mind and life and somehow resulting in human value and biological complexity and order do not cohere.

Besides the known facts that nonliving matter does not come alive and that nothing comes from nothing, atheists are inconsistent in the way they live. When we honestly look at these arguments, weigh them, and judge them according to each other, the only one that makes sense is that there is a Creator and sustainer of reality.

This brief study of the arguments for God's existence are fortunately not exhaustive and are definitely not static. These arguments continue to build and grow along with new discoveries in science, philosophy, and archeology. Surprisingly, arguments for God's existence are not even necessary. It is reasonable to have a basic belief in God just as we believe in history. We are not able to prove that the universe was not created twenty minutes ago, but we know it wasn't. That is a properly basic belief. Belief in God is properly basic and does not require arguments

> since what can be known about God is evidence among them, because God has shown it to them. For His invisible qualities, His eternal power and divine nature, have been clearly seen since the creation of the world, being understood through what HE has made. (Romans 1:19–20)

CHAPTER 14

What Does It Matter?

Implications

Throughout this book, we have ventured through much data and information regarding interesting facts and ideas about the universe and reality. The main point is that there are really just two options for the existence of all of this information—either God exists or He doesn't. That's it. But why does it matter? Well, our eternity is at stake. There are only two eternal things—God and humans. We will spend eternity with the Creator or without.

Jesus commanded us to make disciples of all nations, and we are to use our God-given talents and gifts to spread His special revelation of the gospel through Jesus Christ. The implications of the decision that this universe came from nothing by nothing or was created by God are eternal. Interestingly, God gave us the choice. We are not forced to believe in Him, but that does not change the outcome.

We all have the same data regarding this matter. Everyone is without excuse. We all have been exposed to His general revelation and are responsible for deciding to believe it or not. The atheist will say there is not enough evidence to believe in God, but that is completely misleading. Evidence cannot prove anything. Proof is the interpretation of the evidence. Throughout this book, it has been demonstrated that it is not wise to make a decision based on just one parameter or premise but to build a case for the whole. Some evidence is not as strong as other evidence. But just because one piece of evidence is weak does not decrease the strength of the remaining claims. Taken together, all the evidence with all the explanations and data are best associated with a sufficient and necessary creator.

With the scientific proof of the beginning of the universe and the philosophical conclusions, there does not seem to be any other option. The Flying Spaghetti Monster is atheism's god of the gaps, not the God of the Bible. The naturalists' descriptions and understanding of the God of the Bible are naïve attempts to use schoolyard tactics to try to explain away an idea of the supernatural that makes them uncomfortable.

No matter the vitriol or justifications used by atheists against God, we all have to answer the fundamental questions. Atheism fills the scientific gaps of origin and information with speculation and imaginary numbers. But there is a deafening silence that is unsatisfying when name-calling and flying monsters are used to distract the real questions not answered by atheists. Christianity does the best job at answering the basic questions of life, and we should all attempt to answer these questions. But just as Jesus asked His disciples, the most important question remains, "Who do you say that I am?"

READERS' GUIDE

Chapter 1

1. What is apologetics? Is it necessary?
2. Why is apologetics useful especially in the context of society and culture?
3. Does the lesson of Ignac Semmelweis apply to apologetics and Christians in the politically correct and sensitive culture of today?

Chapter 2

1. What is the role of medicine?
2. Is it internally coherent to be an atheist and a physician?

Chapter 3

1. What are some of the mysteries of medicine, neurology, and God?

Chapter 4

1. Can neurology offer a systematic paradigm for weighing the evidence in reality?

Chapter 5

1. What are the implications of the cosmological arguments for God's existence?

2. Does nothing exist? Can anyone actually think of the absence of anything?
3. Do atheists believe in bigger miracles than do theists?

Chapter 6

1. What is meant by objective morals?
2. Can we just pick and choose our morals as our mood fits?
3. How can an all-loving and all-powerful God allow evil and suffering?

Chapter 7

1. What is meant by the interacting whole?
2. Does the universe actually depend on its constituent parts?

Chapter 8

1. Why do you think naturalists do not want to or cannot search outside the box of the material world to explain reality?
2. What are some examples of fine-tuning of the universe and of our solar system and planet?
3. What is meant by intelligent design? Does it imply creationism?

Chapter 9

1. Do you think the cortical architecture and function can be explained by chance and time?
2. What are the implications of a single protein that is crucial to life and is finely tuned in amount and multiple roles?

Chapter 10

1. What is the mind? Is it a physical thing?
2. Do you think computers will one day be able to make conscious decisions? Will they then have souls as well? Why or why not?
3. How can we explain the placebo effect?

Chapter 11

1. What are order and reliability?
2. How does the order of nature relate to the nature of God?

Chapter 12

1. Does the localization of the nervous system help determine the nature of the creation of the universe?

Chapter 13

1. How can epidemiological studies be used to address philosophical questions?

Chapter 14

1. What are the ultimate implications of what you conclude about these questions?

ABOUT THE AUTHOR

Kris French is a medical doctor of neurology who currently resides in Billings, Montana, and practices medicine at a large hospital. He was trained in neurology at the University of Utah and has special interests in neuroimmunology and the impact of inflammation on the central nervous system. He has published numerous scientific articles in medical publications including the neuromuscular effects of thiamine deficiency in the pediatric population in the journal *Neurology*.

He enjoys studying medicine and Christian apologetics, but he most enjoys activities with his wife, Lindsey, and their two children, Klaire and James, and will do so with their third.

REFERENCES

Adachi, H. T. (1995). cDNA cloning of human cytosolic platelet-activating factor acetylhydrolase gamma-subunit and its mRNA expression in human tissues. *Biochem. Biophys. Res. Commun*, 180-187.

Almeida, T. R. (2004). Afferent pain pathways: a neuroanatomical review. *Brain Research*, 40-56.

Axe, D. (2010). The Case Against a Darwinian Origin of Protein Folds. *J. Bio-Complexity*, 1-12.

Axe, D. (2010). The Limits of Complex Adaptation: An Analysis Based on a Simple Model of Structured Bacterial Poplulations. *J. Bio-complexity*, 1-10.

Baker, M. (2015, July). *ABC Science.* Retrieved from http://www.abc.net.au/science/articles/2015/07/07/4251468.htm

Barlow, G. (1985). *Vintage Muggeridge: Religion and Society.* Eerdmans.

Beauregard, M. a. (2007). *The Spiritual Brain.* New York City: Harper One.

Behe, M. (1996). *Darwin's Black Box.* The Free Press.

Behe, M. (2001). Reply to My Critics: A Response to Reviews of Darwin's Black Box: The Biochemical Challenge to Evolution. *Biology and Philosophy*, 685-709.

Belova, A. S. (2014). Revised McDonald criteria for multiple sclerosis diagnostics in central Russia: sensitivity and specificity. *Mult Scler*, 1896-1899.

Chesterton, G. (1908). *Orthodoxy.* Create Space Independent Publishing.

Chesterton, G. (1910). *What's Wrong with the World.*

Cole, L. A. (2015). The Evolution of the Primate, Hominid, and Human Brain. *J. Primatology*, 124.

Comins, N. (1993). *What if the Moon Didn't Exist?* Harpercollins.

Corbo, R. (1999). Apolipoprotein E (APOE) allele distribution in the world. Is APOE*4 a "thrifty" allele? *Ann Hum Genet*, 301 - 310.

Craig, W. L. (1979). *The Kalam Cosmological Argument*. Eugene, Oregon: The Macmillan Press LTD.

Craig, W. L. (2008). *Reasonable Faith: Christian Truth and Apologetics 3rd Edition*. Wheaton, Illinois: Crossway.

Craig, W. L. (2010). *On Guard; Defending your faith with reason and precision*. Colorado Springs: David C Cook.

Craig, W. L. (2014). *Reasonable Faith*. Retrieved from Defenders 2 Podcasts: http://www.reasonablefaith.org/defenders-2-podcast/transcript/s4-6

Crick, F. (1990). *What Mad Pursuit*. Basic Books.

Curlin, F. e. (2005). Religious Characteristics of U.S. Physicians. *J Gen Intern Med*, 629-634.

Darwin, C. (1859). *On the Origin of Species in the Struggle for Life by Means of Natural Selection*. London: John Murray.

Dawkins, R. (1995). *River Out of Eden: A Darwinian View of Life*. New York City: Basic Books.

Dawkins, R. (2006). *The God Delusion*. Boston: Houghton Mifflin Company.

de Rouvroit, C. a. (2001). Neuronal Migration. *Mechanisms of Development*, 47-56.

Dembski, W. (1998). *The Desing Inference: Eliminating Chance through Small Probabilities*. New York City: Cambdridge University Press.

Dembski, W. a. (2008). *Understanding Intelligent Design*. Eugene, Oregon: Harvest House Publishers.

D'Souza, D. (2007). *What's So Great About Christianity*. Washington DC: Regnery Publishing.

Eccles, J. a. (1984). *The Wonder of Being Human*. Free Press.

Forbes, J. V. (2016). The Gut Microbiota in Immune-Mediated Inflammatory Dieseases. *Frontiers in Microbiology*, 1-18.

Fry, A. C. (2014). The Genetics of Lissencephaly. *Am J of Med Genetics*, 198-210.

Gauger, A. a. (2011). The Evolutionary Accessibility of New Enzyme Functions: A Case Study from the Biotin Pathway. *J. Bio-Complexity*, 1-17.

Gonzalez, G. a. (2004). *The Privileged Planet: How our place in the cosmos is designed for discovery.* Washington, DC: Regenery Publishing, Inc.

Guerrini, R. a. (2014). Malformations of cortical development: clinical features and genetic causes. *Lancet Neurology,* 710-726.

Harrington, A. H. (2010). C. elegans as a Model Organism to Investigate Molecular Pathways Involved with Parkinson's Disease. *Developmental Dynamics,* 1282-1295.

Hawking, S. (2010). *The Grand Design.* New York City: Bantom Books.

Hoche, B. a. (1920). *Allowing the Destruction of Life Unworthy of Life.* Leipzig, Germany: University of Leipzig.

Hoskins, J. (2016). Digital Souls. *Christian Research Journal,* 36-39.

Huxley, J. (1964). *Essay of a Humanist.* Harper and Row.

Kim, D. L. (2015). Botulinum Toxin as a Pain Killer: Players and Actions in Antinociception. *Toxins,* 2435-2453.

Kinnaman, D. (2011). *Six Reasons Young Christians Leave the Church.* Retrieved from Barna Group: https://www.barna.com/research/six-reasons-young-christians-leave-church/

Kreeft, P. (1994). *Handbook to Christian Apologetics.* Downers Grove, IL: Intervarsity Press.

Lewis, C. (1944). *The Problem of Pain.* New York: Macmillan.

Lewis, C. (1949). *The Weight of Glory.* Harper One.

Lewis, C. (1952). *Mere Christianity.* Geoffrey Bles.

Lifton, R. (1986). *The Nazi Doctors: Medical Killing and the Psychology of Genocide.* Basic Books.

Locke, J. (1689). *An Essay Concerning Human Understanding.* London.

Luskin, C. (2015). Responding to Criticisms of Irreducible Complexity of the Bacterial Flagellum from the Australian Broadcasting Network. *Evolution News and Views,* 1-11.

Martin, M. (2007). *The Cambridge Companion to Atheism.* New York City: Cambridge University Press.

Miller, K. (2007). *Finding Darwins God.* New York: Harper Perennial.

Nuland, S. B. (1988). *Doctors: The Biography of Medicine.* New York: Vintage Books.

Ohtaka-Maruyama, C. a. (2015). Molecular Pathways Underlying Projection Neuron Production and Migration during Cerebral Cortical Development. *Front. Neurosci,* 1-24.

Peckham, C. (2015). *Medscape Physician Lifestyle Report 2015.* Medscape.

Penrose, R. (2004). *The Road to Reality. A complete guide to the laws of the universe.* New York City: Vintage Books.

Polman, C. R. (2011). Diagnostic Criteria for multiple sclerosis: 2010 Revisions to the McDonald criteria. *Ann Neurol,* 292-302.

Rasio, F. a. (1996). Dynamical instabilities and the formation of extrasolar planetary systems. *Science,* 954-956.

Rees, M. (2000). *Just Six Numbers.* New York City: Basic Books.

Reeves, M. G. (2014). Enzyme Families-Shared Evolutionary History or Shared History? A Study of the GABA-Aminotransferas Family. *BIO-Complexity,* 3.

Reiner, O. a. (2013). LIS1 functions in normal development and disease. *Current Opinion in Neurobiology,* 951-956.

Ross, H. (1995). *The Creator and the Cosmos.* Navpress.

Russell, B. (1927). *Why I Am Not a Christian.*

Samuel, A. (2010). Aquinas' Cosmological Argument. *The Richmond Journal of Philosophy,* 1-6.

Schreiner, A. K. (2015). The gut microbiome in health and in disease. *Curr Opin Gastroenterol,* 69-75.

Spurgeon, C. (1855, January 7th). *The Immutability of God.* Retrieved from The Spurgeon Archive: http://www.spurgeon.org/sermons/0001.php

Stonestree, J. a. (2015). *Restoring All Things.* Grand Rapids, Michigan: Baker Books.

Strong, J. (2007). *Strong's Exhaustive Concordance of the Bible.* Peabody, Massachusetts: Hendrickson Publishers, Inc.

Truong, D. (2009). *Manual of Botulinum Toxin Therapy.* New York: Cambridge University Press.

Victor, M. a. (2001). *Adams and Victor's Principles of Neurology; 7th Edition.* New York: McGraw-Hill Medical Publishing.

Vilenkin, A. (2006). *Many Worlds in One.* MacMillan.

Wakefield, A. (1998). Ileal-lymphoid nodular hyperplasia, non-specific colitis, and pervasive developmental disorder in children. *Lancet,* 637-641.

Wallace, J. W. (2013, February 22). *Cold Case Christianity.* Retrieved from ColdCaseChristianity.com: http://coldcasechristianity.com/2013/theres-a-difference-between-evidence-and-proof/

Yingling, J. e. (2008). Neuroepithelial stem cell proliferation requires LIS1 for precise spindle orientation and symmetric division. *Cell*, 474-486.

Zacharias, R. (2016, May 13). *RZIM*. Retrieved from Just Thinking: http://rzim.org/just-thinking/must-the-moral-law-have-a-lawgiver/

Zukav, G. (1989). *The Seat of the Soul*. New York City: Simon and Schuster, Inc.

INDEX

71594559R00121

Made in the USA
Columbia, SC
01 June 2017